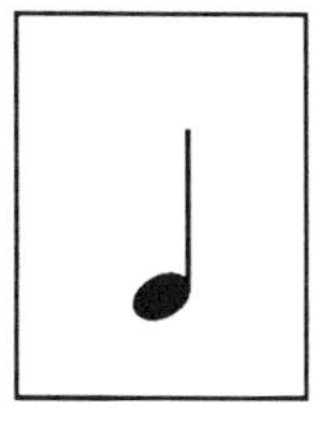
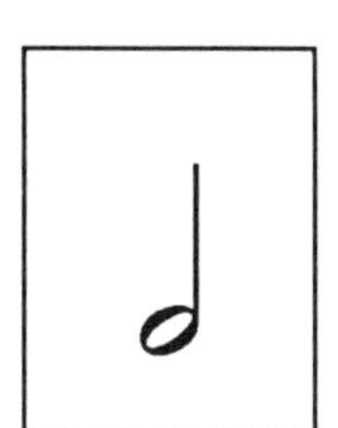

VOICES OF INDUSTRY

MUSIC EDUCATORS NATIONAL CONFERENCE

in cooperation with

Music Educators National Conference
1902 Association Drive, Reston, VA 22091

Printed in the United States of America
ISBN 0-940796-81-3

Contents

Contributors

Michael Bennett is general manager of the Band and Orchestral Division of Yamaha Corporation of America, based in Grand Rapids, Michigan. He is president of the National Association of Band Instrument Manufacturers, president-elect of the Music Industry Conference, and, until recently, was co-chairman of The Music Achievement Council. Bennett is also a member of the board of directors of the Grand Rapids Symphony Orchestra and a veteran of over twenty years in the music industry. He received his musical education at The MacPhail College of Music and at The University of Minnesota, Minneapolis, with graduate study at Indiana University in Bloomington.

Bob Bergin graduated from Texas Wesleyan College with bachelor of music and master of education degrees. His teaching experience includes general music, band, orchestra, and choir at the elementary, junior high, and high school levels. Bergin is president of Rhythm Band, Inc., currently serves as president of the Music Industry Conference, and is a member of the National Executive Board of Music Educators National Conference. He also serves on the coordinating committee for the Foundation for the Advancement of Education in Music and is a past board member of the American Orff-Schulwerk Association.

Jacquelyn Dillon is educational director for the Scherl and Roth stringed instrument division of C. G. Conn Ltd. and editor of the Scherl and Roth publication *Orchestra News*. She has also held several executive positions in marketing and in managing stringed instrument lines in the musical instrument industry. She has presented clinics or guest-conducted orchestras throughout North America and in Europe; as a teacher, she has founded and administered award-winning string programs in the public schools. Her published works include a comprehensive textbook devoted to string-class and orchestra teaching and many articles in publications for music educators.

Bob Dingley was born in Solihull, Warwickshire, England, and grew up in southeastern Texas. He attended Sam Houston State University, majoring in music education. Immediately after leaving Sam Houston State he found himself in the sheet music business. During his twenty-two years in the music industry he has been heavily involved in the evaluation and selection of educational music, both as a publisher and as a retailer. He presently serves as marketing director for J. W. Pepper & Son, Inc., a leading retail source of educational music.

Sandy Feldstein, president and CEO of CPP/Belwin, Inc., is a highly respected performer, composer, arranger, conductor, and innovator in music education. His music, books, and educational software are used all over the world. He has twenty-five years of publishing experience: before joining CPP/Belwin, he was executive vice president of Alfred Publishing Co., Inc. He holds a doctorate from Columbia University, New York.

Charles L. Gary, after teaching in the public schools, has been on the faculty of Austin Peay State College in Tennessee, Purdue University in Indiana, George Mason University in Virginia, and The American University in Washington, D.C., and teaches currently at The Catholic University of America in Washington, D.C. He was a member of the MENC staff for eighteen years, including eight as executive secretary of the conference. Beginning in 1963, he represented the position of music educators and music education associations on the Ad Hoc Committee of Educational Organizations on Copyright, working with the U.S. Congress on the revision of the copyright law.

Beverley Herz started her professional career in retailing and became a buyer for Joseph Magnin Company in San Francisco. She returned to college in 1970 to study the travel industry and decided to pursue a second career in this field. Herz has traveled extensively as a tour leader and travel manager throughout the United States, South America, Europe, and the Orient. She has accreditation from the Institute of Certified Travel Agents and is currently director of sales and marketing at Intropa/International.

Roger McRea is the founder and president of Temporal Acuity Products, Inc., a company with sixteen years of commitment to products supporting music education. He completed undergraduate degrees in music and in business and a master's degree in higher education. He taught junior high and senior high choral music for ten years in the Seattle public schools and served for four years on the music faculty of Foothill College in Los Altos Hills, California. Since 1978, he has devoted his time to the development of products and new technologies in the field of music. He travels extensively as a clinician and participates in workshops with teachers at all levels of music education.

Mike McRoberts has been employed by International Music Company for three years as division director for Akai, a leading manufacturer of digital samplers and digital tape recording equipment. McRoberts majored in music composition at Wichita State University. He was formerly the owner of a recording studio, and produced the first Christmas music tape utilizing entirely electronic instruments.

Craig D. Northrup received bachelor of music and master of music degrees from the Conservatory of Music at the University of the Pacific in Stockton, California. He taught band, orchestra, and choir at all levels in California and Oregon for seventeen years before becoming the managing director of Intropa International/U.S.A. in 1979. During his teaching career he and his performing group covered more than fifty thousand miles of touring through the United States, Canada, and Europe. In 1974, his band won the "Prize of Vienna" for the most outstanding ensemble in the International Youth & Music Festival in Vienna, Austria.

Harry Wenger, as music director for the Owatonna, Minnesota, public schools in 1940, began as a hobby what is now a company recognized as a leading manufacturer of support equipment for music education and performing arts—the Wenger Corporation. In the early years, an innovative sousaphone chair-stand, a new conductor's baton, and a snare drum practice pad made up Wenger's product line. Today, Wenger Corporation offers music posture chairs, music stands, risers, acoustical products, staging, cabinets, and conductor's equipment, in addition to its many customer capabilities.

Preface

The Music Industry Conference (MIC) has served for more than sixty years as a liaison between the music educators of the United States and the manufacturers, publishers, and distributors who provide the materials and equipment used in music education. Growing concurrently with the Music Educators National Conference, the nonprofit MIC continues to work very closely with music educators by providing information on and understanding of the many business-related problems that confront them. The resourcefulness and expertise of MIC members have proven very helpful over the years.

MIC is very pleased to have worked in conjunction with MENC in producing *Voices of Industry*. The MIC members contributing to this effort are recognized by their peers as leaders in their respective areas of the music industry. Our goal in presenting *Voices of Industry* is to share information, insight, and suggestions that might be helpful in providing a good music education for every child. We hope you will find this information to be helpful and thought provoking.

Bob Bergin
Music Industry Conference

Selecting the proper performance music for all performing ensembles is one way to assure the success of any music program. Three critically important aspects of the selection process are explored: knowledge of available music, including suggestions for gathering and absorbing this information; the music itself, including criteria for selecting it, and the relationship between music educators and their music dealers.

Selecting Music for Your Performing Group

by Bob Dingley

Selecting music begins at the source. As far as music educators are concerned, the source may be a music dealer or, in some cases, the publisher. In recent years, many publishers have begun to encourage educators to purchase through music dealers rather than ordering directly from them.

The most important aspect of selecting music is knowledge. Throughout our performing and teaching careers, we come in contact with or have occasion to hear incredible amounts of music. This exposure should provide us with superb performance music choices. If you retain the concert programs for performances you attend, making notes of selections that appeal to you or that may be of interest in the future, you will find this to be an invaluable long-term source of selections.

The information age in which we live assures you of a steady flow of information from many sources. Be sure you are on the mailing lists of publishers and retail music dealers throughout the country. This will assure your receipt of a wealth of publicity materials, including recordings, new product announcements, catalogs, and general information. Music periodicals, including *Music Educators Journal*, *The Instrumentalist*, and *The Choral Journal*, along with the state music educator magazines, provide

---

Bob Dingley is marketing director for J. W. Pepper & Son.

an additional source of music, both in advertising and in editorial materials. Read these magazines regularly to stay up-to-date both on what's new and on what's important.

Also, don't miss any opportunity to attend your state music educator association conferences, national meetings of groups such as the Music Educators National Conference and the American Choral Directors Association, and events such as the Mid-West Band & Orchestra Clinic and the Northwest Band Clinic. These events can provide exposure to music, composers, clinicians, and other directors, all of whom are great sources of information for the performance music you may need. Publisher-sponsored or music-dealer–sponsored workshops and reading sessions can also provide that same exposure. Some nationwide music dealers have now begun to provide prepackaged recorded workshops for use in selecting new music for your groups. If you haven't explored this concept, do yourself a favor and try it.

Considerations in Selecting Music

The next important aspect of selecting music is the music itself. There are certainly many things that must be considered in making the right choices. I will outline some general selection criteria and then offer some specific criteria for the choral, band, and orchestra areas.

Make sure that the music provides reinforcement for all of the music and performance fundamentals that you are teaching throughout your music program. Every performing ensemble should be an enhancement to the overall music education program.

Know your students and make sure the music is relevant to them. This in no way means you have to compromise your educational goals, but it does mean that the interests of your students should be a factor in the selection process. Be aware of your community, and program with an eye toward community awareness. This can be very good for public relations and can help assure that your programs are of interest to your community audiences as well.

Make sure that difficulty levels of the music are within the reach of your students. This may well be one of the most critical areas in assuring the success of your program. Choosing music that offers no challenge may severely limit the growth and progress of individual students, as well as the potential of the entire ensemble. By the same token, choosing music that is beyond the reachable bounds of your group may create a frustration level for students and yourself that may prove defeating. It is important to avoid either extreme and to select music that offers an attainable challenge for your group.

Consideration of standard repertoire and the classics is most important in the development of a well-balanced performance program. However, there are "classics" and then there are *classics.* A few of the tests that you might consider as part of your evaluation process are the following:

- Is the selection relevant in today's world? (Consider this especially in regard to the lyrics in choral and vocal selections.)
- Has the selection stood the test of time? (Some selections have dropped into virtual obscurity—for good reason.)
- Does performance of the material provide enrichment for students and/or audiences?
- Does performance of the material enhance the musical development of your students?

Consideration of pop and current chart materials is also an important aspect of music selection. Pop materials in a music education program provide an ideal link to demonstrate to the students how important music can be as a part of their lives. I have always viewed the use of pop materials with performance ensembles as the dessert topping off a super meal. A little bit is the perfect addition to any program, but a steady diet would be too much. You might use some of the following criteria in examining pop materials for your program.

- Will the fame of the selection and the recording artist that popularized the music be obvious to your students and audiences?
- Will performance of the selection be offensive in any way to your students, your audiences, or any other group?
- Will performance of the selection enhance your program or the public perception of your program?
- Is the quality of the arrangement sufficient to fit within the educational goals of your program?
- Is the selection relevant to your students today?
- Will it withstand even the most liberal test of time?

When it comes to specific performing ensembles, there are some additional key points for consideration in your selection of music. For choral groups, they include the following.

- Are the voice ranges within the levels of your students?
- Do the lyrics work well with the music? (Some works become like tongue twisters when students try to fit the music and lyrics together.)
- What type of accompaniment does the selection require? Do you have access to the required instruments?
- Is the text appropriate for the level of your students?

For bands and orchestras, consider these questions:

- Are the individual parts within the reach of your students? (You should take advantage of the capabilities of strong sections of your ensemble and, possibly, avoid materials that openly feature sections that may still be developing.)
- Be sure to take into consideration the instrumentation of your ensemble when selecting music. (Many directors today find, due to scheduling conflicts, unbalanced instrumentations within their performing ensembles.)
- Be sure that if the selection requires any special performance instruments or equipment you have access to such items.
- For orchestras in particular, be sure, when ordering music, that you order sets that include sufficient string parts for your entire ensemble. The packaging of orchestra sets has been through an evolution in recent years, and it is extremely important to stress the number of parts you require when ordering.

The Music Dealer

The third ingredient in your selection of music must be your music dealer. With the time pressures faced by today's music educators, it is imperative that we, the dealers, ensure that the teachers' time is spent in the most productive manner possible. In choosing a music dealer to assist you in the all-important job of selecting the proper performance music, please consider the following things. All dealers should:

- Provide information about the music that is available. This may be in the form of catalogs, fliers, or brochures.
- Recommend music that might be appropriate for your specific situation.
- Allow you to examine the music before making the purchase.

- Provide exposure to new music through various workshops or special promotional efforts.
- Provide prompt fulfillment of orders and requests for information.
- Keep themselves informed, so that they can keep you informed of news and trends within the music industry that may affect music education.

The relationship between a music educator and a music dealer should be a two-way street and good for both parties. You should let your dealer know exactly what you need and expect from them and settle for nothing less.

As music education is continually changing, so is the music industry. It is important for you to stay informed of changes regarding publishers, distributorships, and the like so you will always know the proper sources of the music you need. While none of us know truly what the future holds, technological changes now enable us to have direct computer links to dealers, utilizing almost any personal computer, to secure information, to place orders, and to exchange information and ideas with other directors. These changes will, no doubt, revolutionize the way you order your music in the future, but the final decision and the most important ingredient in the proper selection of music is *you.* The more informed you are, the more informed your decisions will be, and the better your program will be.

The music equipment teachers select can make a critical difference in the quality of music students learn to create. "Selecting Equipment for Your Performance Group" examines some of the features a music director should look for in music furniture, storage cabinets, risers, staging, and, acoustical products for practice, rehearsal, and performance areas. These features really can and do affect the quality of music at every stage in the learning process.

Selecting Equipment for Your Performing Group

by Harry Wenger

The music equipment you select for your music students can make a critical difference in the quality of music that your students learn to create. High-quality equipment that is specifically designed for music-making purposes can improve the music education process and can even help shorten the learning cycle.

You should always select well-designed, high-quality products that will minimize long-term costs and maximize the value of your investment: this is true of music stands, chairs, storage cabinets, risers, staging, acoustical products, or products for any other music-specific need. The equipment you select should be engineered to last for decades, to offer enduring good looks, and to be both aesthetically and acoustically compatible with your music facility. Let's examine some of the features an experienced music director looks for.

Music Stands and Chairs

Music stands, because they're in constant use, need to be durable and trouble-free. You shouldn't have to worry that repeated bumping, banging, and dropping will loosen a stand's desk or base. Look for music stands with permanent welded

---

Harry Wenger is president of the Wenger Corporation.

bases, heavy-duty desks, and rolled edges—or the tough, colorful, new polystyrene desks that protect instruments from damage. Look for stands that allow easy adjustment of height and that stay adjusted. Look, too, for stands that come with transport and storage carts that allow convenient storage and life-enhancing handling.

The posture provided by standard school chairs isn't always good enough—you intend to make great music. In music, the chair becomes an extension of the musician's body, and as such, it profoundly affects a student's posture and breathing as well as his or her comfort and attentiveness. For that reason, music departments demand more from seating than just about anyone else in education.

A properly equipped music room requires specially engineered chairs that can help enforce ideal posture for music makers. Ideal posture can mean less stress on the lower back, more evenly distributed weight, fewer pressure points, and—most critical for the musician—easier diaphragmatic breathing. This can in turn allow students more volume potential, greater breath control, and a more conscious command of the music they create.

When replacing music room chairs or adding to those you have, consider these key features: the chairs should be designed by a music specialist, not just by a classroom chair resource who modifies a feature or two and markets it as a "music" chair. Posture chairs should be further specialized to meet the needs of specific types of musicians: for example, a chair may accommodate the unique half-sitting, half-standing posture of a string bass player; may be a specialty chair for the cellist, percussionist, tubist, or sousaphonist; or may even be a conductors' podium-desk-and-chair ensemble designed for the special needs of directors. Getting the right seating with the right specialized features can mean more control and better visual and aural access to students. For students, the right type of seating can mean better concentration and better skill development with less effort spent handling the instrument or getting into position for proper breathing.

Cabinets

Proper storage and handling of sheet music, garments, instruments, and other musical necessities can make a big difference in how long you can expect these investments to last. Storage cabinets especially designed for music applications offer the best protection of your investments in the tools for making music. Look for cabinets built from wood products (the noise of metal locker-style cabinets can be very distracting). Look for cabinets with polyethylene shelves that won't splinter like wood, won't show wear, and are gentle on instruments, cases, and garments. Look for garment cabinets with plenty of ventilation and hanger spacing—this can keep dry-cleaning costs to a minimum while it keeps uniforms and robes looking fresh and wrinkle-free.

Look for instrument cabinets with an assortment of compartment sizes, allowing the best use of space. You can even have a set of instrument cabinets designed by computer to specifications that match the instruments in your band or orchestra. In placing the cabinets, you should design cabinet-area floor plans to minimize traffic-flow problems at the beginning and end of rehearsal.

Modular cabinets offer the benefits of custom, built-in units plus the flexibility to move, add to, and reuse cabinet components as needs change. In addition, there are a number of rolling cabinets on the market for storage of music folios and stringed instruments. Also consider wall-mounting brackets to store large instruments safely out of the way and lockable rolling storage and performance centers that allow you to take percussion instruments or an entire music department's electronics equipment to other locations in your school. Look for casters that let you move heavy equipment with ease and for protective edges that resist bumps and dings. A family of matching cabinets that attractively meets all your storage needs can be ideal.

Risers

Risers are another music room basic that should be selected for quality and durability. Because risers elevate the student, they can have a surprisingly positive effect on your musical group's ability to achieve ensemble. Students are better able to hear the sounds around them and better able to blend and project music, for a more finely tuned overall effect. Students are also better able to see you and take their cues.

Portable choral risers are ideal for traveling groups, while modular riser platforms and roll-away–style risers allow easy setup, quick changes between acts, and convenient storage. Risers with a reversible step design can accommodate a variety of straight, winged, or semicircular formations. Choose a riser that stands securely on stationary legs rather than casters, that stores compactly, and that has carpeted steps for minimum noise. Look for well-engineered connector hardware that unites sections into a single, stable system.

Modular seated-style risers, which accommodate chairs, let you modify the music room as needs change. Hardboard seated-style risers with closure panels offer a built-in look and can actually enhance room acoustics. Because the risers are portable, you can move the risers into the performance area, which gives you one more measure of control and allows the sound to be more consistent.

Staging

Staging is another equipment item that can influence the quality of music. A well-designed, creatively set stage not only lets performers look their best and feel more confident but can enhance the projection of sound.

A number of modular staging styles can cost-effectively modify and improve existing built-in stages or offer innovative staging possibilities for new or remodeled performance halls. Modular staging can be used to set up permanent or temporary stages of all sizes, shapes, and elevations. It can be an ideal way to convert an unused pit into an expanded stage that puts performers in closer touch with their audience; it can also be used to form runways to span permanent structures such as hillsides or fountains—to create a customized stage for the special needs of performers and your audience.

Quality is a central issue when choosing staging. Look for staging units with structural members that are bolted, not screwed, for maximum reliability. Look for load-tested units that are engineered for highly stable, trouble-free setup and compact storage. Look for staging that can also facilitate drama, dance, gymnastics, and other disciplines.

Acoustics

The acoustical treatment in a music facility is probably the most obvious and most complex equipment need of all, and acoustical considerations begin where the music education process begins: in the practice room. When you consider acoustics, performance areas immediately come to mind, but don't overlook practice and rehearsal areas. Shortcomings in the acoustics of the areas in which you teach daily can have a permanent impact on the developing musical skills of your students. In the practice room, sound must be adequately isolated to keep it from spilling over into adjacent classrooms, making those areas undesirable learning environments. In addition, practice room acoustics should provide an accurate representation of sound over the entire spectrum, so students can learn to hear and improve their music.

Prebuilt, self-contained practice rooms offer a known solution to practice needs. These rooms can be installed in a few hours. They are designed for their specific acoustical qualities, are available in a wide range of sizes, and offer your music department the flexibility to add or relocate practice areas at any time.

At the next stage of music education—in the rehearsal room—acoustics become more complex. Here, the students must learn to blend their own sound with that of others for a richer, coordinated effect. In addition, you need to be able to hear and direct each student in the room. Good rehearsal room acoustics require a balance of sound-absorbing and sound-diffusing surfaces (surfaces that absorb and control loudness or boominess and surfaces that diffuse or distribute sound, especially delicate high-frequency sound). The more balanced acoustics can be in rehearsals, the more successful your performances will be.

In new construction, proper room size and layout are major acoustical factors. Other factors in new construction, as well as in renovations and less-involved room improvements, include the choice of floor, wall, and ceiling materials; the fact that graduated concrete floors decrease the actual room size and increase the loudness in the room; and the fact that carpeting, draperies, and other absorptive materials may actually intensify a low-frequency acoustics problem by readily absorbing already hard-to-hear high-frequency sound while having little effect in controlling boomy bass sounds.

In an untreated rehearsal room, low frequencies are often so overpowering that dynamic contrast is difficult to achieve, articulation and phrasing details are obscured, and musicians find it nearly impossible to hear themselves or other sections of the group clearly. In an acoustically balanced rehearsal room, loudness is controlled, communication among musicians is good, and you as the music director receive an accurate impression of the ensemble's balance.

The most practical and economical way to balance rehearsal room acoustics is through the application of a strategically located system of acoustical wall and ceiling panels. Identifying the correct set of acoustical panels for a given application can be surprisingly easy and cost-effective. For more comprehensive rehearsal room needs, an acoustical consultant or architect may prove your best resource. Another good resource is the book by Harold P. Geerdes, *Music Facilities: Planning, Equipping, and Renovating,* which is available from the Music Educators National Conference.

Finally, the performance area, the acoustical environment in which every music director is ultimately judged by an audience—is the acoustical environment in which you may have the most at stake. An acoustical shell can help minimize shortcomings of a proscenium-type theater. Without a shell, much of the sound can be lost to sound-absorbing materials in the upper stagehouse and wings before it is heard even by the performers—and long before it reaches the audience! With a sound-reflecting shell surrounding the musical group, the music is reinforced. The group's members can better hear themselves and can better project the music they create.

Shells are available in a variety of types, from economical traveling models, to roll-away shell sections, to full-stage and custom enclosures, audience clouds, and wall-and-ceiling acoustical systems that integrate the stagehouse and audience house into a single, superior acoustical environment. For these more complex treatments, an acoustician or architect can be a school's most reliable resource.

There are many factors that affect the way your student's music will sound. By selecting the most appropriate products and equipment, you can maximize your control over the factors that affect musical quality. Perhaps the most important consideration of all is your choice of a reliable product resource. Find a supplier who has both the knowledge to help you identify the most appropriate products and equipment for your application and a reputation for successfully supporting the similar needs of others in the field of music education.

A concert tour can be a great motivator for students in performing ensembles, building enthusiasm among students and their parents. Properly organized, a tour can also present a wonderful educational opportunity for your students. "Planning a Successful Concert Tour" presents ideas about planning, organizing, and funding a concert tour, notes on selecting a tour operator, guidelines to use during the course of the tour, and a discussion of some potential "pitfalls" and how to avoid them.

Planning a Successful Concert Tour

by Beverley Herz and Craig D. Northrup

Another study year is ending. The final concerts were outstanding, and you and your ensemble received well-deserved congratulations for a fine performance. Plans for summer break will soon crowd out the memories of long hours of practice and rehearsal culminating in the exhilarating sound of applause and cheers. But what happens when the students return next semester? What incentive will encourage your well-trained musicians—and those soon to step into the role of seasoned performer—to return to your program?

There is no better incentive for a well-developed performer to continue in the program than the dream of a concert tour in the near future. Of course, the decision to tour with your group is an extremely important one, requiring not only a good deal of preparation but also a solid backing of support. Let's examine this decision a little closer. It's important to know where the idea originally started and why, since this is a good indication of how much support you have for the idea of a tour.

The idea may have been a suggestion from the students. The group may have toured before or perhaps have heard about the tour of a neighboring ensemble, or you may have hosted a tour-

---

Beverley Herz is director of sales and marketing for Intropa International. Craig D. Northrup is managing director for Intropa International/USA.

ing group that has reciprocated with an invitation to visit them. The idea may have begun with an invitation to a festival or another special event (an excellent reason to plan a concert tour), or finally, you may simply have made your plans because you realize the opportunity that touring affords the students. You know it will expand their horizons and serve to keep their interest high throughout the year, while it will offer worthwhile musical and educational values.

So let's take a look at what goes into the planning of a concert tour. First and foremost is the determination to see your idea through its planning stages to the realization of a dream come true— both for you and for the students.

Planning

Support for a tour must come, first of all, from the school administration. Most school administrators acknowledge the benefits of a well-organized tour. Your main responsibility as director, naturally, is the further development of your students' skills. You must, therefore, be able to organize dependable committees to help with the details of the trip, and you must be available to guide and encourage the volunteer team and to keep control of the direction of the plans.

You must have the parents' support and cooperation in order to achieve success in these efforts. The parents, in turn, must realize the importance of teamwork: you should establish a board of directors, responsible for selection of the tour operator and organization of committees, if one does not yet exist. The two most important committees to establish immediately are the finance committee and the rules committee (more committees can be added later when the need arises). These two groups should comprise both parents and students. When setting down rules of procedure and conduct, it is important for adults to listen to the students' input in order to achieve their cooperation while on the tour. The students will also be an important part of the fund-raising efforts.

Selecting a Tour Operator

The most important decision to be made is the selection of a tour itinerary and the company that will organize the concert tour. When selecting a company, consider first that company's *experience.* Ask how long they have been in business and request names of groups that have toured recently with the company. Check references thoroughly.

Also consider the company's *knowledge.* Always choose a company that specializes in concert tours: this type of tour requires unique coordination only achieved through many years of experience. Any travel agent can arrange a sightseeing tour—only a concert tour operator can successfully arrange a concert tour.

Next, consider *professionalism.* The tour company should be approved by the American Society of Travel Agents (ASTA). The company should have in their employ travel agents accredited by the Institute of Certified Travel Agents (ICTA), indicating their successful completion of a certified travel counselor degree in tour and travel planning. In addition, the company should be fully bonded and insured.

Establish that the company offers *competitive and realistic pricing.* Of course, you must always compare "apples" with "apples" when analyzing the costs of the tour. Be certain to compare prices for tours with the same:

- Number of days and nights included in the tour.
- Type of transportation. Costs may differ depending on the class of train tickets (first or second, reserved seating); the type of bus used (deluxe touring, air-conditioned); the fact that you use a scheduled airliner charter flight; or the type of airfare used (be sure you know the restrictions and cancellation penalties).
- Hotel accommodations (class of hotel, how many per room).
- Number of meals included.
- Services supplied. Ask how the company interprets the terms "tour guides," "tour escorts," "tour leader," and "tour operator."
- Publicity. Compare the preconcert publicity plans offered to assure you of good audiences for your concerts.

Also, if this is an international tour, choose a company that maintains an office in the country you plan to tour. Finally, always insist on a contract that spells out all details clearly. Read it carefully and be sure you understand all details.

Some Pitfalls

Beware of cutting costs too much. In travel, as in anything else, you get what you pay for. Everyone wants something for nothing, but we rarely get it. One example is the providing of "freebies" for staff and chaperones. Don't kid yourself. The tour operator builds the cost of those who don't pay into those who do. If you want the lowest cost for the students, don't ask for a lot of freebies. It is generally accepted that the director will go free, and, in large groups, the director's spouse and/or the accompanist may also go free.

A word about hotels: In some parts of the world, less expensive hotels do not include a private bath or shower. This is a necessity for most Americans. You don't want to rough it when traveling and performing. It only costs a few dollars more per night to have private facilities, and this should be included, at least for the majority of the trip.

Beware of promises of transportation via chartered flights. Everyone has heard horror stories about cancelled flights, poor service, and being packed in like sardines when using some charter services. Again, you get what you pay for. Charters can cancel as little as a week before departure for any reason with no more than a refund to you. With a charter, it is impossible—even two months prior to departure—to find alternate reservations for groups. Scheduled departure and arrival times for charters are approximate. Several hours' delay at the airport for no apparent reason can be an exhausting way to start or end a tour. And yes, charters usually squeeze as many seats as possible into the aircraft. Most charters charge extra for shipping instruments and uniforms.

In today's world of competition among airlines, a good tour company will be able to find discounted airfares on a regularly scheduled airline with guaranteed departures. Be sure you understand the rules connected with the type of airfare proposed. There may be as many as a hundred different airfares between any two major cities, and each of them has different rules regarding changes and cancellations.

Choose the tour that is right for your group. It may be that your ensemble performs well in adjudication and enjoys the competition. Or perhaps you would like to emphasize the sharing of talent and music through cultural exchange. A visit to a "sister city" usually insures the interest and support of both cities' governments and business officials. Homestays are a possibility that should be discussed among the members of the group. Your ensemble may enjoy participating in a joint concert with a local group with similar interests in the area you plan to visit. In any event, your reasons for embarking on the tour should be reflected in the itinerary finally accepted. Although it is impossible to completely please everyone, each participant should have some input regarding the itinerary.

Since some questions will arise once the itinerary is accepted, the tour operator must have a toll-free number for your easy access to needed answers. Always ask for references from groups that have traveled recently with the tour operator, including names and telephone numbers. Follow through and check them out. Be sure to ask about preconcert publicity and the quality of tour escorts provided by the company. With the right questions at hand, it should be easy to "weed out" the inexperienced or unprofessional companies. Choose a company with which you will feel comfortable and confident in assuring your ensemble a most successful concert tour. If you want excellent concert venues and contact with local musicians on an international tour, it is imperative that your tour operator maintain an office in the countries that you will be visiting.

Fund-Raising Ideas

Your tour operator should be able to suggest many methods of proven fund-raising activities. An experienced operator can supply you with many pages of ideas that have worked successfully for groups similar to yours. Each group will find ideas that will create enthusiasm and cooperation, so that the fund-raising becomes an exciting part of the preparation.

The key to raising money is *publicity*. Notify your local newspaper of your upcoming concert tour. Be sure to keep this goal and your related activities constantly before the public. In this way, when someone is approached for help, they will already know about the plans.

Assigning Responsibilities

You, as music director, should be in charge of coordinating the trip. However, your major responsibility should be *music*. One of the chaperones should be designated as the "tour director." It should be the tour director's responsibility to supervise all non-musical aspects of the trip. Following are some of the jobs that should be the responsibility of specific chaperones—not the music director:

- Rooming: When checking into a hotel, one chaperone should have a roommate list ready. This person will pick up all the keys and assign rooms. Everyone waits for room assignments *on the bus* while the unloading crew unloads luggage. Any changes of roommates or rooming assignments are worked through this person.

- Curfew: Each and every chaperone should check to see that the students he or she is in charge of are in their rooms at the specified time and should then report to the bed-check coordinator.
- Medical problems: These should be taken care of by a nurse, doctor, or parent with some medical background. This person should carry completed medical release forms for each student, and must be aware of any chronic medical problems.
- Attendance: Bus seating assignments and attendance-taking procedures are important at each loading or unloading of the bus.
- Pictures: You will need a photographer to take still photos and videos of each performance. Everyone will want copies! Have a big show when you return and take orders for copies (of course, you will need the appropriate permission from the copyright holders of the music you perform). Another future fund-raiser!
- Equipment: Assign a manager to see that all luggage and equipment is accounted for. This person is also responsible for supplying a list of all musical equipment, including size and weight of containers, to the tour operator, who then notifies the airline and the bus company.
- Assistant conductor: A musical assistant should be assigned (if possible) to conduct performances if you become ill.... Heaven forbid, but the show must go on.

With these guidelines, your next concert tour should be a positive experience that all participants will treasure for the rest of their lives.

"Getting a Child Started in Instrumental Music" explores the process the potential student goes through in being introduced to the music program as well as influences that can positively or negatively affect the student's progress. For both educators and parents, Michael Bennett discusses the considerations involved in choosing a dealership. These considerations concern the ability of a dealership to provide sales and service, not only after the student obtains a beginning instrument but throughout a student's musical career.

Getting a Child Started in Instrumental Music

by Michael Bennett

Children are selected to participate in instrumental music programs in one of several ways. Some school districts and instrumental music teachers use predesigned, standardized music aptitude tests. These tests are designed to identify children having natural abilities in the field of music. The tests, however, do not identify on which instrument the child will be most successful or guarantee in any way that the child will be successful if he or she decides to play a musical instrument. The test is only an indicator of natural music abilities.

It's important to note here that virtually all children have some level of God-given ability to participate in musical activities. However, not all children will be interested or motivated to try to play a musical instrument. Children scoring at the average level or above on music aptitude tests are usually encouraged to try musical instruments. Also, a balanced instrumentation in the band or orchestra may be a critical factor in determining which instrument the teacher recommends for the child.

Another method for selecting the child for a particular musical instrument is the *trial lesson program.* In this program each child is allowed to come to the instrumental music specialist and to try

---

Michael Bennett is general manager of the Band and Orchestra Division, Yamaha Corporation of America.

each instrument that will be offered. Then the teacher lines up the child's instrument preference with the instrument on which the child exhibited the greatest amount of success and decides with the child what specific instrument he or she should try. This system can be used in connection with the music aptitude test.

Student profiles are another way of selecting children for instrumental music. Student profiles are usually done in chart form and have places for the classroom teacher, the classroom music teacher, and the physical education teacher to evaluate the child in their specific fields. This method attempts to identify academic excellence, interest in music, and the physical skills of the child. Once this is studied by the instrumental music teacher, he or she can better focus the child towards a specific instrument.

Another method for recruiting children on musical instruments is the actual *physical demonstration* of the beginning instruments. This is done in a variety of ways, including demonstrations by teachers, demonstrations by high school players, and demonstrations by other elementary children. This method allows the potential beginner to hear firsthand the sound of the instrument of his or her choice. Ultimately, instrumental music teachers attempt to interest and encourage all grade-school children and their parents to take advantage of the opportunities offered in instrumental music. Recruiting letters are usually sent home to parents informing them of the testing program and encouraging them to allow their child to begin on a musical instrument. Usually these letters contain a suggestion of a specific instrument for the child.

Keys to Successful Participation

The real key to a child's successful participation in instrumental music is *interest maintenance.* Maintaining and supporting a student's interest in instrumental music brings together four groups of people. The first group is the parent-family group. The second group is the teachers. In this category we not only include the music specialist that teaches the child but all other teachers that influence the child's learning activities. The third group is the child's own peer group; the fourth group of people involved in interest maintenance is made up of the music dealers that provide the instruments for rental or sale.

It is in the best interests of all of these these groups to support each other and the child in the endeavor to learn a musical instrument. When these four groups function in harmony, the child is provided with a pleasant and positive learning situation. What can each of these groups do?

The parent-family group can praise the student for his or her accomplishments, regardless of how small these accomplishments may be. Taking a sincere interest by listening to the lesson being prepared and encouraging the child is critical. The parents must also stress the importance of daily practice and good practice habits. Providing an area for the student to practice, removed from the distractions of the household, will also enhance learning. Finally, it is necessary to maintain an instrument in the best playing condition possible to ensure good performance. Parents should be sure to provide the child with the proper cleaning and maintenance items so the child can, in fact, do this.

The teacher group plays a unique role in the support of the child's successful participation in music. The classroom teacher's positive attitude and support of the music lesson and ensemble program plays a large part in the child's attitude towards music. The other member of this group, the music specialist, is the key person in the teacher group. The music specialist supports and critiques the child in a very positive way and moves the child forward towards success. This teacher group and the school environment directly influences our third group.

The child's peer group plays a large part in the child's attitude towards music. We must remember that the children not involved in music can negatively influence those children who are striving to learn and be successful on an instrument. All of us must work together to create positive attitudes in all children towards music.

Today's music dealers realize more than ever that they are part of the overall plan for the child's successful participation in music. Providing quality instruments and innovative rental programs for parents is the music dealer's primary function. Children cannot compensate for poor-quality instruments; such instruments can directly affect their motivation to practice and can cause poor performance.

Selecting a Music Dealer

When selecting a music dealer, a parent should look for a store that can do more than service their immediate needs. Ask these questions:

- Does the music store provide the rental plan that the music instructor is recommending?
- Does the dealer explain the rental plan well?

- Do rental fees apply to the purchase price of the instrument?
- Are there finance charges built into the program, and if so, what are they?
- Does the music store provide routine service to the school on a weekly or biweekly basis?
- Does the dealer offer a private lesson program? Are free lessons included in the rental price?
- Does the salesman that provides the service to the school keep the teacher supplied with updated information in the music education field and the music industry?
- Does the music store have the ability to deliver a "shop from home" service to your school and to you as a parent?
- Does the music dealer have the ability to do repairs? Make loaners available? Deliver the instrument back to the school?
- Does the music store offer a coverage for loss, damage, and repair to the rental instrument? If the dealer does offer this, does it include coverage on your invested rental dollars?
- Does the music store offer an extended maintenance plan for the instrument once the instrument is purchased?
- Does the music store offer workshops to music teachers that will provide them with current teaching materials and ideas? This service can be at no charge to the educator.
- Does the music store offer educational support systems affecting both parents and students?
- Does the music store provide the reputable brand-name instruments the music teacher recommends?
- How long has this store serviced this school? Are other parents satisfied with their service? Are the instrumental music teachers satisfied with the service?
- Does the music store have available the necessary materials to assist your child, such as method books, solos, and ensemble literature? How about important accessory items, such as reeds, mouthpieces, lubricants, and maintenance kits? Virtually all serious school service dealers have these items readily available.

Intermediate and Professional Instruments

This category deals with the ability of the music dealer to care for your long-term needs. Again, evaluate the dealer by asking:

- Does the dealer have a wide selection of intermediate instruments that you can look at as the child progresses?
- Are the dealer's prices competitive?
- Does the dealer's "on approval" service bring those instruments to the school so that the child can try them at the school?

For the beginning parent, it is difficult to properly evaluate the services a good music dealer provides. Value takes time to determine, but if the time is taken to obtain answers on the aforementioned questions, sound decisions can be made that will affect the success of the child in a positive manner.

Studies show that instrumental music develops fine, creative, responsible, self-motivated children and also serves to help children develop organizational skills. Successful instrumental music students typically perform better than other students in so-called basic academic subjects such as math and science. They develop self-confidence and learn a sense of teamwork that will help them as adults— both in the workplace and as parents themselves. These skills and traits last a lifetime, and the opportunity is available to all children. All they have to do is sign up and join the band or orchestra.

String teachers can develop support for the school string program by working with and educating their students' parents. Jacquelyn Dillon supplies teachers with answers to parents' questions and concerns, a rationale for the study of stringed instruments, and a brief list of some of the opportunities open to string players. She also explains the parents' role in providing good-quality instruments and constant encouragement to help ensure each child's success.

How to Educate Parents for a Better String Program

by Jacquelyn Dillon

As a string teacher, you probably have success recruiting lots of students who want to play, but you must also use your recruiting skills to reach the children's parents. Parents can be the music program's best allies—but *only* if they are informed about what it is that you are trying to do with your students and why your work is important. You should inform parents of these facts frequently, from the time students consider playing an instrument until the time that they leave you.

Meeting the Parents

Many schools schedule an evening meeting for parents and students at which they can discuss beginning the study of a stringed instrument. If your school has never done this, you might contact the teacher of a successful program in your area for hints about organizing such a meeting. You can also obtain materials for recruitment from many manufacturers and distributors of stringed instruments: those companies that are members of the Music Industry Conference are listed every two or

---

Jacquelyn Dillon is educational director for the Scherl and Roth stringed instrument division of C. G. Conn, Ltd.

three years in the *Music Educators Journal* (see the March 1988 issue).

Parents should come at a set time, so that you can talk to all of them at once. After talking to them as a group, give the parents a chance to talk to you individually so that you can help the parent and child make a definite choice of an instrument and determine the instrument's size. This will keep you busy, so you may need to ask another knowledgeable string player to help you with this meeting.

You will encounter some students who want to play but whose parents were unable to attend or not interested in coming. A parent who fails to attend may be concerned about his or her child's level of talent or commitment, about adding to already crowded music schedules, about the relevance of music to future careers, or about the perceived difficulty of stringed instruments. Although it may be time-consuming, a telephone call answering these concerns can usually turn this parent around.

Remind the parents that all students have some degree of talent, and that all children need to explore a variety of activities— the child may develop a strong commitment to playing a stringed instrument. Tell the parents that a student who participates in other areas of music has an excellent background for faster learning of the instrument than his or her classmates, and that children who excel in academics can also learn to play relatively quickly— they already know how to make good use of their time. Finally, remind parents that even three-year-olds can, with proper teaching, learn to play stringed instruments correctly and successfully, producing recognizable tunes with good tone quality in the earliest stages of study.

Rationales

Obviously— as far as we string teachers are concerned— the most important reason for a child to participate in the school orchestra is to know the joy that comes from playing the vast repertoire of orchestral music. Sometimes, however, this statement has very little meaning to prospective parents, so you need to discuss other benefits a child can obtain by participating. For example, playing an instrument:

- Makes a person feel good; it gives pleasure and fills the need to create something beautiful
- Builds confidence and self-esteem
- Makes a person feel proud and special; it sets him or her

apart from the ordinary
- Fills the important need to be accepted; allows the student to belong to the circle of friends so important to adolescents
- Provides an opportunity for leadership
- Teaches teamwork and cooperation
- Channels energies into worthwhile pursuits
- Develops concentration; it promotes the ability to work out details patiently and diligently
- Develops coordination between the hands as well as between the mind and body
- Teaches young people to enjoy the challenge of working toward set goals

Before concluding your conversation with parents, tell them that most students who play instruments do well in academics and are leaders in many other school activities. Mention also that what students learn from playing a stringed instrument will apply to other areas of school life and, even more important, will help them in later life. Studying music never hurts—in fact, it enhances and beautifies students' lives while teaching them lessons necessary for success in any career.

Opportunities

Parents are most interested in knowing what the opportunities may be for their children's future. Stress to them that opportunities for a string player are unlimited—whether those opportunities are in the guise of a career or as a rewarding leisure-time activity.

For example, almost all colleges and universities make scholarships available to string players who play in the college orchestra—whether or not the player is a music major or a major in another field. Some of these scholarships can be quite sizable; to qualify, students generally need to study privately and to participate in the school orchestra, as well as in youth symphonies, string ensembles, and orchestra festivals.

Almost all communities have orchestras that welcome string players with open arms. Some professional or semiprofessional groups require more skill, but one can almost always find an orchestra sponsored by the city, county, university, church, or temple in which less-advanced string players may feel comfortable. These groups often include players of all ages and from many career fields; string players tend to play throughout life because it is relatively easy to maintain the technique necessary to perform successfully on these instruments—and the joys of playing are addictive.

Another popular area is that of small groups or ensembles. Those who want to play "classics" usually play in string trios, quartets, and so forth, but pop string ensembles and "strolling string" groups are growing in popularity in both schools and communities. These groups most often play lighter music—everything from pop, to rock, to country or bluegrass, to jazz.

Teaching is a wonderful, rewarding career for string players to consider as either a full-time or a part-time career. Public school teaching, which requires a degree in music education, opens unlimited opportunities throughout the United States; salaries are quite good and the work is professionally and emotionally satisfying. Many teachers continue to play in professional groups and teach privately while they pursue their public-school teaching careers in our country's ever-increasing number of string programs.

The Parent's Role

Once the parents have made the decision to let their children play, you need to educate them about their role in ensuring their children's success. In the beginning, the two most important areas that you need to discuss are those of *providing a good instrument* and of *encouraging the child.*

Before the parents go out to seek instruments, you should give them a set of recommendations. You can send them these ideas by letter (many teachers attach a separate page about securing instruments to the recruitment letter; ask colleagues for ideas or sample letters) or discuss the points in your evening meeting. Be sure to mention the following:

- Parents should rent or lease the instruments for at least the first year. Most school music dealers offer rental plans with an option to buy once the parent is ready to make the commitment.
- Parents should follow your advice about local music dealers that have good-quality beginner instruments for rental. You may want to list acceptable brand names. Advise parents to avoid purchasing an instrument from a department-store catalog. A catalog instrument may be of uncertain quality and will probably not be backed up by a knowledgeable service and support staff.

- Be sure that the instrument is the correct size for the student. Most beginners cannot start on full-size instruments, so the instruments are available in graduated sizes, some very small. If the instrument is too large, the child will be uncomfortable and will not want to practice.
- Tell parents to beware of instruments found in pawn shops or attics: these instruments will probably be of inferior quality, improperly sized, and neither equipped nor adjusted to play properly. Make certain that they don't try to save money by asking the child to play on Aunt Sarah's violin: by the time parents pay for necessary repairs on an old instrument, they will have invested more than the instrument is worth and exceeded the rates charged to rent or lease an instrument from a local musical instrument dealer.

The Instruments

Good-quality *beginner* instruments, called student-line instruments, should be shop-adjusted in the United States and follow the MENC minimum standard specifications. These can be found in detail in the MENC publication, *The Complete String Guide*. All student-line instruments should have an ebony fingerboard and properly fit ebony pegs, a good-quality bridge that is fitted to proper shape and height, four good-quality steel strings with adjusters, a good-quality fiberglass or wood bow with fresh hair, a good-quality, sturdy case or instrument bag, and a new cake of rosin.

Once the child is ready for a full-size instrument, parents should be strongly encouraged to upgrade to a "top-line" instrument. Student-line instruments, designed to be sturdy and to withstand the heavy wear and tear imposed by beginning students, cannot produce the kind of tone needed for the more mature music played in middle, junior, or high school orchestras.

Top-line instruments are made from much better quality wood, are more carefully carved and graduated, and more of the work on them is done by hand. They are thus able to produce more volume and a better-quality tone. Top-line instruments should be equipped with more expensive strings made from wound gut or perlon, a good brazilwood or pernambuco bow, and better accessories and case or bag. Most school music dealers with good rental programs are willing to help parents in the upgrading process by applying much of the rental from the small instrument to the purchase of a better instrument. As a teacher, you must continually remind the parents of the importance of a better instrument for more advanced playing, letting them know that students will be judged on tone in future auditions for select groups.

Keeping Students Playing

When students get discouraged, it is sometimes not because of a lack of success but because they lack parental support and interest. Often, parents do not realize that they have great influence on the success or failure of their children's musical endeavors. Some children get a bit discouraged after the newness of the instrument has worn off and they are starting to learn something that is a bit more difficult; let the parents know that their encouragement at this point is of utmost importance. Early in the game of teaching students to play, tell the parents such things as:

- Take an interest in your child's playing. Ask questions, and have the student demonstrate what he or she has learned. By all means attend concerts and let your child know how proud you are.
- No matter how bad your child's playing may sound, say encouraging things such as, "You are sounding better, but I hear a spot that doesn't sound quite right. Are you sure you are doing it exactly as the teacher wanted?"
- Don't make judgments. If you are not sure how your child is doing, ask the teacher. Remember that it takes time to learn anything, and be patient.
- Provide a quiet place for practice, away from the distractions of others and the television.
- Let the teacher tell you how much practicing is expected. Don't feel that your child is not learning because you have to remind him or her to practice. This is normal—children don't relish practicing, just like they don't like to clean their rooms. The teacher will let you know if your child needs more practice. Don't tell your child that he or she has to practice a certain amount of time unless the teacher asks for it.
- Expect the child to play for an entire school year before deciding about continuing to study. By the end of the year, the school group will sound good, and the wonderful feeling of making music with others will be a part of your child's life.

Welcome parents to the wonderful world of strings early in their children's careers. Let them know that they are in for a wonderful time as the parents of string players—and that they will be amazed at how much their child will be able to play at the end of just one year, and amazed at what playing can do for a child's self-confidence. Then keep in touch with the parents as your students—their children—progress. Send friendly progress reports home from time to time.

Good luck; your job is not an easy one—it is truly a labor of love.

Musical experiences involving instruments during children's early years are important and full of positive ramifications. Children must have both good instruction and good instruments, and a multitude of good percussive and melodic instruments are available to teachers and students for music instruction in today's marketplace. Bergin identifies appropriate instruments for preschool through grade three as well as sources for instructions and guidelines.

The Role of Instruments: Preschool through Third Grade

by Bob Bergin

The enthusiasm, boundless energy, and eagerness to learn that are so evident among the preschoolers with whom I have been in contact over the years have always been a source of interest to me. Preschool children are vivacious, full of life, and for the most part uninhibited. They long to have the opportunity to express themselves in song. This desire to express oneself in song, when nurtured at an early age, can lead to a lifelong musical experience that results in happiness and provides a means of self-expression.

The child's first introduction to music is usually through lullabies sung by parents, grandparents, brothers, and sisters. Radio and television also have a strong influence on children, because music assumes such a major role in commercials and programming. Children learn numerous songs by rote and go about singing these songs during playtime as one means of expressing themselves.

Parents, preschool teachers, and church or temple staff members should all plan their time with children to include sufficient

---

Bob Bergin is president of Rhythm Band, Inc.

time for guided listening activities as well as structured, "hands-on" music experiences. Children love these activities, which are a wonderful way to foster group interaction and self-expression. Music becomes richer, more meaningful, and more usable, however, when it is learned in a planned, structured manner—especially when instruments are played by the participants. Playing musical instruments helps to make music come alive.

Playing, Participating, and Developing

Singing is enjoyable, but playing an instrument adds a very special dimension to music, stimulating a desire for personal involvement and participation by everyone. Once stimulated, this desire for participation in and through music will continue to resurface over and over and over again.

In addition to bringing about unlimited enjoyment, playing a musical instrument has been shown through research to improve a young person's level of intelligence. George Anderson, supervisor of music for the Saginaw, Michigan, schools between 1965 and 1980, did extensive research with preschoolers through grade six, with follow-up testing over a fifteen-year period. The results of his research indicate that young people's I.Q. scores improved by ten points if they played a musical instrument.

Ella Jenkins, an idol of children over the years, continues to be recognized and admired by children of many nationalities for her gift of song, which she has shared through singing and playing the baritone ukulele and rhythm instruments in workshop and concert settings around the world. Part of the mystique surrounding an Ella Jenkins workshop or concert is the crowd participation that seems to come about so naturally. In no time at all everyone in attendance is responding to the music through the playing of instruments, singing, and movement. I can vividly hear in my mind Ella singing the words, "Play your instruments and make a pretty sound."

Ella, and many teachers and artists like her, have concentrated their teaching and performance endeavors on preschool and early grade levels, because they believe a good foundation for music appreciation and music participation must begin in these early years. Children who are exposed to music early in their lives—and who are given the opportunity for active participation by way of actually playing musical instruments—usually have a lifelong meaningful experience with music.

Creating and Purchasing Instruments

Children love to create and to listen to the multitude of sounds that result from the playing of different rhythm and melodic instruments. Innovative teachers will quite often encourage and help students to create their own personal musical instruments. This is a wonderful activity for home or school, one that children enjoy and of which they never seem to tire.

In addition to making their own instruments, children, parents, and teachers can purchase a wide variety of instruments designed for successful use in early childhood through music stores, school supply companies, and catalog houses. It is very important that children only be exposed to safe instruments that are structurally sound, that do not use toxic paint or have sharp edges, and that will provide good service over a long period.

It is always wise to purchase from a reliable company that has a good reputation for dependability, honesty, and after-the-sale service, and a good track record of being supportive of music education. Of course, I must admit I am prejudiced and would encourage you to purchase from firms who are members of the Music Industry Conference. These firms are also members of the Music Educators National Conference and have proven their interest in and support of music education. You will find members of MIC, listed every two or three years in the *Music Educators Journal* (see the March 1988 issue), to be reliable and ethical in their business practices.

Instruments and Instructional Methods

Instruments used from preschool through grade three are usually divided into two main areas—*percussive* and *melodic.* Instructions and guidelines for playing rhythm instruments are readily available through a multitude of sources. The major textbook companies recognize the importance of including lesson plans and instructions for playing rhythm instruments in their music series. Silver Burdett & Ginn; Macmillan; and Holt, Rinehart & Winston all emphasize rhythm instruments in their textbook series and provide excellent instructions targeted not only for the music specialist but also for the classroom teacher who has little, if any, musical expertise. This is important because unfortunate budget cutbacks in school systems in many parts of the country have adversely affected the staffing of schools with music specialists at the elementary-school level, and more and more elementary music instruction is being done by classroom teachers.

Another excellent source of music instruction at the elementary school level is the *Music Young People Can Do* series by Howard Doolin. This combined instrumental and vocal approach to music instruction, which may be started at virtually any age, requires no prior musical skills or understanding. It is also used successfully by classroom teachers as well as music specialists. The third book in the series, *Building A Rhythmic Foundation*, is an organized compilation of rhythmic studies and activities that deal specifically with duration of tones, which are coordinated with a collection of songs. Doolin suggests activities designed to encourage people to respond to rhythmic content of the music and to begin reading notes and symbols representing duration of tone.

The Suzuki method is also an excellent preschool/elementary approach to instrumental instruction that continues to receive wide acceptance and provides excellent results.

An excellent handbook with practical information for teachers who want to use music with special education students is *Music for Special Education* by Martha Slyoff. The recommended activities and sample lesson plans included are very helpful for teachers who have not had previous experience working with handicapped people.

Playing rhythm instruments has many useful purposes— mental stimulation, enjoyment, physical exercise. It's a great activity for early childhood and for special education of all ages, and may also be used very effectively with the aged and with nursing home residents.

Percussive Instruments

There is a wide range of percussion instruments available, from very basic, inexpensive rhythm instruments to very sophisticated, high-priced instruments. One of the unique advantages of working with young children is that basic rhythm instruments are suitable and children love to play them. And, equally important, a large expenditure is not required to place instruments in the hands of all the children in the group.

Some of the more common instruments included in the percussive instrument category are drums, woodblocks, sand blocks, tap-a-taps, rhythm sticks, handle castanets, finger castanets, hand castanets, jingle taps, triangles, claves, cymbals, nonpitched bells, tambourines, hand drums, snare boys, tom boys, cowbells, shakers, bongos, congas, maracas, guiros, temple blocks, gongs, roto-toms, slit drums, and other special-effects instruments such as bird whistles, African squeeze drums, cabaças, flexatones, ratchets, and hand chimes.

Percussive instruments are usually played on the beat and help children to feel the rhythmic pulse of the music being played or sung. They may also be used to emphasize special accents in the music. Many of these instruments may be used very effectively in special education and in some instances may be adapted for use by people with physical problems. Examples would be larger knobs for easier grasping of sand blocks, tap-a-taps, triangles, cymbals, and woodblocks. Headless tambourines are much easier to grasp than tambourines with heads. And if a student isn't able to grasp at all, he or she can usually still produce rhythmic sounds with wrist, loop, or ankle bells.

The attitude of the teacher, leader, or activity director is extremely important. If those who play the rhythm instruments are encouraged to realize they are playing "real" musical instruments, and not toys, their musical experience will be much more meaningful and enjoyable.

I am quite often asked by classroom teachers and beginning music teachers to list materials that are useful in introducing rhythm instruments at the early childhood level. The following is a compilation of very basic materials designed for successful use with preschool through grade three.

- *Rhythm Band Fun* by Ken Mulkeroy includes suggested procedures for developing original rhythm scores.
- Another very basic book, *Ella Jenkins's Rhythm Fun*, explains how to play the various rhythm instruments.
- Joan Hillsman's book, *Afro American Music Concepts with Rhythm Band Accompaniment*, provides a basic introduction to blues, jazz, ragtime, spiritual, and gospel music with suggested activities and sample scores for rhythm instruments.
- *Rhythm Band for Little People* is an excellent early childhood rhythm band program in which children read rhythm symbols on large charts and play instruments simultaneously with recorded music.

Chording and Melodic Instruments

Chording and melodic instruments may also be introduced quite effectively and successfully at the preschool level. Most preschoolers quite naturally enjoy music and can't wait to have the opportunity to learn to play melodies on instruments. Some of the more prominent chording and melodic instruments that appeal to preschoolers through grade three are Chromaharp or Autoharp, soprano ukulele, keyboards, tuned diatonic and chromatic bell sets, recorder, and Orff instruments such as glockenspiels, metallophones, and xylophones.

Quite often Chromaharps or Autoharps are introduced at the early childhood level because they are so easy to play and immediate success is obtainable. To play the instrument, the performer has only to press a chord bar down and strum the strings with a pick or finger. Most Chromaharps and Autoharps are equipped with either fifteen or twenty-one chords and provide a sufficient selection of chords to play literally hundreds of songs. It's not only a good accompaniment instrument; it can also be used to play melodically. Jill Trinka, Jewel Boesel, Becky Blackley, and Meg Peterson are recognized throughout the United States for their effective and inspirational Chromaharp/Autoharp workshops for teachers. Attend one of their workshops and you are sure to get turned on to these unique instruments!

One of the least expensive ways there is to teach the piano keyboard is to use accurately tuned diatonic or chromatic bells sets. The key words here are *accurately tuned.* It is important for children to hear exact pitches from the beginning so that they will be able to identify correct as well as incorrect intonation. Chromatic bell sets are organized in a piano keyboard format with white and black note bars laid out accordingly.

Glockenspiels, metallophones, and xylophones that are used effectively in the Orff approach to music instruction also have their note bars organized in a keyboard format. Children find the various tone colors available from the various Orff instruments to be very interesting and enjoyable.

Other instruments that can be used to teach piano keyboard are melody horns, pianacas, and melodicas. Sound is produced on these instruments by blowing through the extension tube or mouthpiece at the same time you press one or more notes on the keyboard of the instrument. There are also battery- and adapter-powered portable keyboards available that are relatively inexpensive and provide an excellent way to play songs on instruments with a piano keyboard format. I highly recommend selecting keyboards with polyphonic capability rather than monophonic. Children should be able to play chords as well as melodies.

The most widely used melodic instrument by preschool through elementary school players is the soprano recorder. This is an excellent preband instrument that has a two-octave chromatic range and makes possible the playing of thousands of songs. More and more teachers are now including recorders in their instruction instead of flutophones, tonettes, and song flutes, which only have a one-octave range, play terribly out of tune, and which students quite often think of as toys. Students think of recorders as real musical instruments, and rightfully so.

When purchasing recorders, it is very important to select a brand that is engineered to produce correct intonation, good tone quality, and easy response on the instrument's low C. For beginners, I also highly recommend selecting a recorder with a built-in thumb rest, as this will automatically place the right hand in the correct playing position and provide sufficient support for balancing the instrument. The recorder should also be manufactured in one piece, provided it plays in tune. This ensures that students will not be tempted to move the separate pieces and adversely affect the intonation. There are many recorders on the market that do not provide adequate intonation and tone quality. Don't purchase these instruments. It is much better to pay a little more and have a top-quality recorder that functions properly and that will provide many years of good service.

Plastic recorders, which are much better than wood instruments for the early years of playing, are very inexpensive and durable. The manufacturers' top-quality brands also offer two- and three-piece soprano recorders for more advanced players. Some of these brands also have available complete recorder consorts including sopranino, alto, tenor, and bass instruments.

Shaping Students' Development

Susan Kenney, a well-respected early childhood specialist and staff member of the music department of Brigham Young University, Provo, Utah, stated in an October 1989 article in the *Music Educators Journal,* "Music educators have long suspected that consistent musical experiences during children's early years may influence not only their future musical growth but their emotional and creative development as well." I fully agree, and believe there can be no doubt concerning the importance of children being exposed to and involved in music during the early years of their lives.

Teachers and parents have available in today's marketplace a multitude of good percussive and melodic instruments for the early years of music instruction. Parents expect—and children deserve—top-quality instruction. It is also important for children to be exposed to top-quality instruments. Good instruction and good instruments go hand in hand and can make a world of difference in a music program.

References

Doolin, Howard. *Music Young People Can Do.* Rhythm Band Publications (PO Box 126, Fort Worth, TX 76101, telephone 817-335-2561).

Hillsman, Joan. *Afro American Music Concepts with Rhythm Band Accompaniment.* Harris Music Publications (PO Box 1356, Fort Worth, TX 76101, telephone 817-457-4632).

Jenkins, Ella. *Ella Jenkins's Rhythm Fun.* Rhythm Band Publications (PO Box 126, Fort Worth, TX 76101, telephone 817-335-2561).

Mulkeroy, Ken. *Rhythm Band Fun.* Harris Music Publications (PO Box 1356, Fort Worth, TX 76101, telephone 817-457-4632).

Slyoff, Martha. *Music for Special Education.* Harris Music Publications (PO Box 1356, Fort Worth, Texas, 76101, telephone 817-457-4632).

Winter, Joan. *Rhythm Band for Little People.* Kimbo (Box 477, Long Branch, NJ 07740, telephone 201-229-4949).

Electronic instruments are increasingly important in traditional music education. Mike McRoberts discusses the various types of electronic musical instruments available and their functions, indicating what equipment is required for an electronic music system and how a composition can be prepared with electronic equipment. The taped version of this discussion features examples of various electronically produced sounds and demonstrations of how they can be used in a musical environment.

Electronic Music and Education

by Mike McRoberts

Electronic music and electronic musical instruments have been developing steadily over the last sixty years and rapidly over the last twenty years. In the last five years, developments in electronic music technology have led to a literally revolutionary way to produce music. They have changed the way music is composed and performed for television, radio, and film. This new technology centers around MIDI, Musical Instrument Digital Interface, an acronym so common now that it is used as both a noun and an adjective. As MIDI technology has progressed, the prices of equipment using this technology have fallen dramatically to well within the budget of a school music program. And MIDI can be used as a powerful tool for teaching the basics of music.

Let's face it. It gets harder and harder to entice young students into traditional music education programs when we live in a world of compact disc players and MTV. Students grow up exposed to electronic musical instruments every day. By adding these instruments to a school music program, you stand a much better chance of arousing and maintaining your students' interest in the program. These instruments can provide a strong foundation in the basics of music.

Mike McRoberts is director of the Akai division of the International Music Company.

Background

When I speak of electronic music in education, I am not referring to the esoteric composition of avant-garde music incorporating synthesizers—I am speaking of the use of electronic musical instruments in a traditional music education setting. When synthesizers first appeared on the music scene in the 1960s, they were large, forbidding contraptions that were so expensive that only large universities could afford them. Furthermore, it seemed that they could only be understood by a handful of users who had more training in electronics and mathematics than in music. But out of this first group of users came progressive thinkers who had the goal of making this obscure technology more accessible for the average musician. As a result, the 1970s saw the development of simpler, preset synthesizers, and finally polyphonic synthesizers capable of producing more than one note at a time. Also during the 1970s, the arrival of integrated circuits (ICs) brought down the cost of everything electronic and made compact synthesizers a reality.

In the late 1960s and 1970s, a very popular instrument among rock groups was the Mellotron (or Chamberlin). This instrument used a large number of loops of magnetic tape that had recordings of real instruments, such as strings and flutes. Each key on the instrument activated one tape loop with a single pitch. Towards the end of the 1970s, a group of Australians reproduced this type of machine using, instead of tape loops, sounds that they recorded digitally into an eight-bit computer. Once the sound was in this form, it could easily be manipulated by computer software. The technology of digital sampling was born.

MIDI Development

In the early 1980s, a group of musical instrument manufacturers met and decided to develop a common interface among different brands of synthesizers. This became MIDI: Musical Instrument Digital Interface. MIDI was conceived primarily as a standardized way to connect a cable between different brands of keyboards, giving each keyboard the capability of playing the other keyboard. Looking towards the future, however, the developers of MIDI included a number of features that could be implemented at some later date, particularly through the use of personal computers. They also developed a unique system of addressing each keyboard in a MIDI system with a channel number, not unlike a television set on which you can select which channel to watch.

Since some synthesizers had keyboards that could sense the velocity with which the player hit a key and use that capability for control of dynamics, MIDI included the ability to transmit this information. Some keyboards could bend the pitch of a note with a special lever or wheel, so MIDI was designed to transmit that information. Other keyboards had a number of preset or programmable sounds available, so MIDI was allowed a method to select those sounds. For composers, a system of recording notes against a timing source, or clock, running at a particular tempo was allowed; this system developed into the sequencer. And last, but not least, MIDI allowed parameters describing sounds to be transmitted among instruments with similar capabilities. This led to the development of computer sound-editing software.

MIDI in the School

Now that you have a basic understanding of the development of MIDI and electronic musical instruments, what does it mean to you? Incorporating a MIDI system into your school excites students to join your music program—they want to learn to make the sounds they hear on television and radio. It allows you to teach the basics of music theory on contemporary instruments. It offers ways of teaching advanced concepts of arranging and orchestration and allows your students to *hear* their fully orchestrated compositions. It better prepares your students for careers in the music industry, and finally, it enhances *your* understanding of contemporary music.

To get your electronic music program started, you're going to need some electronic musical instruments. These fall into several categories. The first category is that of synthesizers. A synthesizer allows you to create new or artificial tone colors from scratch or to use preset sounds. A great deal of popular music heard on records today incorporates synthesizers, so your students will definitely be aware of this type of instrument. Synthesizers are classed as analog (which use conventional circuitry to create sounds), or digital instruments (which use computer circuitry). Analog synthesizers are said to have a "warm" and "fat" sound, while digital synthesizers are said to be "clear" and "bright." In reality, analog and digital synthesizers can offer timbres that are either similar or radically different from each other. Synthesizers are good for producing brass, string, orchestra, and electric–piano type sounds. The sounds are not natural, but they offer an excellent resource for adding texture to a composition and can provide a variety of special-effects sounds.

The second type of electronic instrument that you'll need is the digital sampler. The sampler is an instrument that actually records and plays back the sounds of real instruments (in fact, samplers can record and play back *any* sound). For example, let's say your school music program doesn't have the money for a bass clarinet. A sampler, played from a keyboard, can provide a sound that is virtually identical to that of a real bass clarinet. The same sampler could be used for enhancing the sound of your brass or string sections, and particularly for adding sounds that your band lacks. The sampler is primarily used as a tool for simulating acoustic instruments.

Another instrument that is very important for teaching, particularly for maintaining the students' interest, is the drum machine. The drum machine allows kids to create sounds, actual samples of real drum sounds, that are used in much of today's music. These sounds are activated by striking small drum "pads." By doing this in time to the clicking of a metronome, you and your students can create various drum patterns or rhythms. The drum machine, in addition to keeping the students excited, is also a powerful tool for teaching the elements of rhythm, since students can use it to experiment with different rhythm patterns, including nonstandard time signatures.

Controlling and Transmitting Information

To control your electronic music system, you will need a MIDI keyboard. This can be attached to or be part of either a sampler or a synthesizer, but it must have a MIDI input and a MIDI output jack. The MIDI jack is a five-pin connector that is similar to the DIN connectors on older stereos. A MIDI cable, with five-pin connectors on each end, is used to connect the various pieces of MIDI equipment. You should try to get a MIDI keyboard (synthesizer or sampler) that is multitimbral: that is, one that has the ability to reproduce more than one sound at a time. For instance, you can use a multitimbral keyboard to produce the sound of a trumpet, violin, and bass simultaneously. Most of the synthesizers and samplers on the market today are multitimbral.

Probably the most important item you need for your electronic music system is a digital sequencer. Before the age of the sequencer, music students would write their music down and then hopefully find someone to play it. But in a school band program, or even at the college level, that is not always practical or realistic. If students are to hear their music played properly by a traditional performing group, performers must spend many hours of rehearsal—hours of rehearsal that aren't available in a school music program.

The digital sequencer serves as a sort of recorder or arranger for your students' musical ideas. Using a MIDI keyboard and a sequencer, your students can perform the composition into the sequencer and hear an instant and correct playback. This is an extremely valuable tool, as it allows your students to hear what they are doing. Thus, it can be used for teaching the concepts of orchestration and arranging. The sequencer, when used with a multitimbral synthesizer or sampler, will allow your students to hear *all* the parts of a piece played with different instrumental sounds. Sequencers are available either as computer software programs (particularly on Macintosh and Atari computers) or as stand-alone devices. The advantage of a software sequencer is that it can be combined with your existing computer and quite often can be integrated with other music programs to give you a printed copy of your music. The advantage of a stand-alone sequencer is that it is portable and quite often easier to learn and use.

Finally, you will also need some type of amplifier and speaker combination. You can use headphones, but as we all know, music should be heard and shared. If nothing else is available, your instruments can play back through an existing stereo system—but treat the system gently.

MIDI allows you to transmit and record on up to sixteen different channels. This means that it is possible for you to have up to sixteen different tone colors sounding simultaneously. To reproduce the different sounds, you must either have up to sixteen different keyboards, each set to a different MIDI channel, or a multitimbral synthesizer or sampler. Each different tone color is assigned a different MIDI channel; by using different MIDI channels, your students can record one instrumental part at a time, each on a particular channel, and hear that part played back with its correct timbre. For instance, violin sounds might be on MIDI channel 1, flute on MIDI channel 2, electric piano on 3, and so on.

MIDI allows you to connect different devices, such as a drum machine and sequencer, together. In fact, the drum machine is actually a sequencer that is dedicated to recording and playing back drum sounds. Since you want the drum parts to be synchronized with the other instrumental parts, the drum machine and sequencer can be exactly synchronized via MIDI. The drum machine will usually have a number of "drum pads" that the student strikes to control the sound. While the drum machine is in the "record" mode, it will record the drum beats your students compose and will even correct mistakes in timing by rounding them off to the nearest selected note value. This feature is called "timing correct" or "quantization"; most sequencers have the same ability to correct timing errors.

Creating the Music

What is the procedure for creating music on this system? First, it's best to start with a drum beat. Remember that one way of keeping your students' attention is to create music that is contemporary, so start with a simple rock beat on the drum machine. Make sure that your sequencer and drum machine are synchronized, so that they start and stop together and have the same tempo. After recording the drum part, set your synthesizer to a bass sound, and assign that sound to MIDI channel 1. Let the student record the bass part. Next, choose another sound, perhaps electric piano, and record it onto another MIDI channel in the sequencer. Keep adding parts, using samplers to simulate acoustic instruments and synthesizers for other sounds, until the composition is done or until you run out of sounds. When the students are done and hit the play button on the sequencer, they will hear an instant playback of their composition, complete with different instrumental parts.

After recording the music, you can use the sequencer to manipulate it easily in various ways. You can speed up or slow down the tempo without changing the pitch. (Try *that* on a tape recorder). You can transpose the key of the entire composition up or down without changing the speed (another trick you can't do with a tape recorder). Perhaps best of all, you can reorchestrate the music. Once the music is recorded into the sequencer on different MIDI channels, you have the ability to completely change the synthesizer or sampler sound playing on that MIDI channel. If a particular sound doesn't work, have your students choose a different sound for that part—and reinforce the elements of arranging and orchestration through practical application while sparking the interest of your students and keeping their creative juices flowing.

Flute
Oboe
Clarinet
Bassoon
Violin I
Violin II
Cello
mf
mp
mp
f
f
p
p
f
Fl.
Ob.
Clar.
Bssn.
Vln. I
Vln. II
Vcl.
mf
mf
cresc.
p
cresc.
mf
cresc.
f
mp
f

Samplers, by their ability to reproduce traditional instrumental sounds, can be used for creating "classical" compositions. A multitimbral sampler could play string, brass, and woodwind parts simultaneously. Under normal circumstances, your students would not be able to hear their compositions played back by an orchestra, but with the sampler and sequencer they can hear their "classical" compositions performed so that they can evaluate their efforts. This, of course, will greatly stimulate their desire to study the characteristics of individual orchestral instruments.

Printing

There is another tremendous advantage to teaching with MIDI. With the aid of a computer, many sequencer parts can be printed out in standard music notation. The score on the preceding page is a printout of a twelve-bar composition that was composed directly on sequencer software and then printed out with the help of a music notation program. This may seem to bypass traditional methods of teaching music notation, but in actuality it gives your students instant printed feedback and actually reinforces their training. In reverse, you can type in the music one note at a time from a handwritten manuscript, and then hear it played back for evaluation. Using this type of system teaches the concept of time signatures, measures, rhythm, counterpoint, and all the other facets of making high-quality arrangements. Notation software linked with sequencer software is another outstanding tool for increasing your students' comprehension of standard music theory. Music must be heard to be music; it is not simply dots on a piece of paper.

The real advantage of an electronic music program for you, as an educator, is the enhancement of your ability to attract students with contemporary instruments that they are used to hearing on radio and television. Before they know it, you are combining this new technology with traditional music education training. You're still teaching the fundamentals, but you are doing it in a way your students can relate to better. And your students come out winners, too. They have the rare opportunity to hear fully orchestrated compositions. They can hear and learn from their mistakes in composition and orchestration. It helps better prepare them to be the professional musicians and composers of the future.

Look into it. And thank you for being a music teacher.

Computers, electronic pitch- and rhythm-training devices, MIDI-standard instruments, and electronic composing/performing software are important resources in today's music classrooms. These "teacher's assistants" can help amplify the effectiveness of music educators by handling certain instructional tasks and providing consistent interactive feedback. "Technology in Music Education" reports on available software and hardware and offers tips on obtaining and maintaining educational technology for the contemporary school environment.

Technology in Music Education

by Roger McRea

When you hear the word "technology" these days, it usually means that there are computers involved. As I prepare this description of the exciting possibilities of the computer in the music classroom, the world of computers is changing constantly— so some of the information may not be absolutely current when you read it. I'll try, however, to concentrate on broad ideas that will remain constant and to describe products that will be available for years to come.

New products and programs will continue to appear, but don't let the possibility of some promised future development keep you from getting involved with the wonderful things we can already do. If you start *now*, you'll be ready to take full advantage of anything new in the future, and at the same time you'll be helping your students improve their skills and musicianship *today*.

You know, computers are fantastic! You can use them to help compose, print, and perform music. You can use them to manage a whole string of administrative tasks such as grades, attendance, music filing, concerts, fund-raising, and dozens of other essential things. Finally, you can use computers to teach music. There are two main reasons why you should put computers to

---

Roger McRea is president of Temporal Acuity Products.

work in your classroom: First, you get an assistant; and second, your students get more training.

I'll bet you'd like to be able to teach a lot more musical skills in the time you have available—some ear training, some sight singing, some basic theory such as scales, key signatures, and chords, and maybe even some part-writing. But how could you work all these things in and still keep up with your rehearsal and performance commitments?

You can do it by putting the computer to work. As your assistant, the computer can guide students individually or in small groups through learning tasks you choose for them, while you concentrate on working with your performing ensembles. You'll find that computers have some very special abilities. For example, a computer can give a student immediate feedback on the questions: Is this note in tune or not? If not, how far off is it? Looking at the meter on an electronic pitch-training device, beginning students get the answer when they can do something about it—at the very moment they can learn the most from the experience.

Also, you can be sure your computer assistant will be teaching well, making consistent presentations to student after student—without getting tired or irritable, without taking shortcuts or forgetting to make key points, and without getting called to the phone.

You'll find one of your new assistant's greatest contributions will be in developing music literacy. For decades, we have been sending students off to music schools and finding that, after eight to ten years in elementary, junior high, and high school music programs, they still have had to enroll in remedial sight singing, ear training, and theory courses—just to learn the rules for playing the game. Think how much more these students could accomplish if they came to their professional schooling already trained in the basics and ready to begin advanced work. Ear-training and sight-singing skills don't have to wait for college—they can be mastered as early as the fifth or sixth grade and can be taught by computers.

Just imagine how much fun it would be to work with junior high and high school performing groups for which intonation and rhythmic problems simply didn't exist—groups for which you started in developing ensemble and interpretation skills right away! To help you understand how, let me introduce you to the basic materials that can make all this possible.

The world of computers is divided into two parts. *Hardware* is the physical equipment such as keyboards, screens, disk drives, and tape players. These are like instruments and music stands—they don't change. *Software* comprises the programs that tell the hardware what to do. These programs are like sheets of music that change from piece to piece but sit on the same music stand and are played by the same instruments.

Hardware

The hardware tools used for teaching musical skills range from "dedicated," single-purpose instruments to multi-purpose "general" computers that can be programmed to perform many tasks, and on to computers connected to work together in groups called "networks."

The software for dedicated instruments is often presented on stereo cassette tapes. These devices offer great flexibility in instruction of such skills as rhythmic performance, intonation, and sight-reading, with programs ranging from beginning to advanced/professional levels. Because these devices have a single purpose, they can produce outstanding musical results.

General computers can be quickly adapted to several useful tasks. For example, simply by changing a program disk, a general computer can be transformed from a patient partner for key signature drills into a clever inventor of music dictation exercises.

The Apple II is the present-day standard for general computers in the classroom. The Apple Corporation's commitment to education has been very high over the years. We have found that they were always careful to be sure each new model of the Apple II they introduced ran earlier Apple II series software, and we expect the Apple II to hold its numerically dominant position in the schools for quite a long time. So you won't have to worry that the programs you buy won't have a computer to run them.

If you don't yet have computers in your music department, the Apple II is definitely your best bet. There are more Apple II+ and IIe models out there than any others, and the newer IIgs model is beginning to show up in great numbers. For musicians, the IIgs is nice because it has a music synthesizer built in, but it isn't necessary to abandon older computers as new ones become available. For example, upgrading an older IIe by adding a 3 1/2-inch disk drive and a digital-to-analog converter board (which generates sounds) makes it almost the equal of a brand new IIgs for purposes of teaching musical skills with today's mature Apple II music software.

To focus on one aspect of change, understanding what Apple has done with respect to DOS changes is important. The Apple II has used two different forms of disk operating system (DOS), and both of them will work on all Apple II models. The older DOS, version 3.3, is still used by many educational software producers, but software based on the newer ProDOS, or Professional Disk Operating System, is a must if you plan to use your computers in networks or with higher capacity storage systems such as 3 1/2-inch disks and hard disks.

At one time, all programs were distributed on the familiar 5 1/4-inch floppy disks. They're still very popular, so it's important to consider having at least one 5 1/4-inch disk drive with each computer. The newer 3 1/2-inch disk, however, is both considerably smaller and holds about 5 times as much information as the 5 1/4-inch floppy. The 3 1/2-inch disk is considered standard for the IIgs, and many ProDOS-based programs are available in 3 1/2-inch format. So, while it's still optional, it would be a good idea to equip your computers with 3 1/2-inch drives as well.

Disks and Networks

People who use computers a lot usually end up installing a hard disk drive, which allows them to store the equivalent of 140 or more floppy disks in a sealed unit that never requires disk changing. In the Apple world, hard disks are still way too expensive for schools to be able to provide one for every classroom computer. They are very popular, however, in networks—systems in which many computers are tied together to a "dedicated file server" (a single computer with a hard disk containing all the programs that the students will use). We see many schools installing Appletalk computer teaching labs: these networks are especially powerful because computers all over a building can be connected to a single file server with small, easy-to-install cables.

Networks have a lot of advantages for teaching. They provide a central source of programs, they eliminate disk handling, they allow every student to have access to every program with no waiting, and they make record-keeping a dream. A 5 1/4-inch diskette may hold one program and maintain 100 student records, and a 3 1/2-inch disk may hold ten major programs and maintain about 300 student records, but a hard disk at the center of a network can hold all of the programs used in every department and maintain over 32,000 student records—and still have room to spare.

We expect the Apple II computer to hold its dominant place in the schools for a long time. But two other computer lines that will be important in schools are the IBM-PC (along with its many compatibles) and the Apple Macintosh. While there is presently less music instruction software available for these computers than for the Apple II series, software developers may begin to produce new material for them as they become more widely available in schools. If you have access right now to older Commodore, Atari, or Radio Shack computers, you should be aware that some software companies have translated their music programs for use with these models as well as the more widely used Apples. All in all, however, if you are just now starting to shop or scrounge for computers, you'll definitely have the greatest set of options for teaching music with the Apple II line.

MIDI

An acronym for Musical Instrument Digital Interface, MIDI is an international standard for interconnecting electronic musical instruments and other devices from different manufacturers. If you've been shopping for synthesizers, samplers, sequencers, or other electronic musical devices, you're probably familiar with the term. Many MIDI devices work with general-purpose computers, and most of them contain their own microprocessors for producing and manipulating sounds.

MIDI is certainly technology of the highest order, so it definitely belongs in this discussion. But until now, its impact has been more in the area of performance than in instruction. We believe that MIDI will begin to play a larger role in teaching as the technology matures and new software becomes available. Because of the computer power that's needed to handle compositional programming along with the control of synthesizers and sequencers, future MIDI needs will go beyond the capability of the Apple II. Most MIDI applications require an IBM or Macintosh. You can have access now to mature music teaching programs with your Apple II computers, but for MIDI, you'll eventually need another computer.

Software

On the software side, there is a relatively small number of companies offering music teaching software in the United States (several are listed at the end of this chapter). Watch the technology column in the *Music Educators Journal*, and scan the music technology journals for reviews and reports on new music teaching software and suppliers. Wherever you may locate music teaching materials, I urge you to purchase only instructional software that has been prepared by music education professionals—software that has been designed to relate solidly to the music curriculum. I firmly believe that software authors should be music educators first and programmers second if their products are to be truly useful in the classroom.

An exciting new category of music software has emerged in the last couple of years—music printers. These programs give composers, arrangers, teachers, and students the means to write music on the computer screen, print it out on standard printers, and even play it back, fully orchestrated, through MIDI-connected instruments. Some of these programs are so open-ended and flexible that they give total freedom in page style and layout. They will transpose music automatically and even extract individual parts from the full score. And the newest versions even allow musicians to "play in the notes" from a MIDI keyboard, yielding written musical notation without your ever having to pick up a pencil.

As an example of the teaching versatility of today's Apple II computers, there are currently available a wide variety of programs in:

- ear training, including melodic, harmonic, and rhythmic dictation and error detection
- instrument tutors that teach fingering patterns for different instruments
- music fundamentals, including drills for learning pitches, key signatures, scales, and chord construction
- symbols, vocabulary, and history, reviewing important facts and terms
- playback and composition, with sophisticated programs for composing music, printing publication-quality copies, synthesizing sounds, and for playing the finished product

Some programs are available with student record-keeping functions, so that every time a student works with a lesson, his or her file is dated and time-stamped, and a chronological scoring record is kept. In this way, when teachers want to check on student progress, they simply call up complete records by student name right from their station. Also, network versions will soon include total curriculum management systems in which teachers, by making a few entries on a computerized planning screen, will be able to prescribe for each student a custom-tailored path of lessons selected from all the programs available in the master file.

Budgeting

If you're intrigued with the prospect of using today's technology to improve music education for your students, then the next step is to obtain the equipment and teaching materials to make it all happen. This takes money—and music department budgets are often already stretched to the limit. So before you rush out to the computer store and place your first big order, try these three ideas:

- The Apple II line has been on the market for more than ten years, and many older Apples have been replaced by newer machines. Send out the word that you need these computers. Many parents and business people will be happy to donate them to a good cause.
- Scour every department of your own school or district for Apples that are already retired or about to be. Check the math and science departments, the business department, and all the offices where people use word processing, data base, and spreadsheet software. You'll find a lot of these departments looking at new Macintoshes or IBM-type machines. "Negotiate" for the units they're replacing. One of the best ways to negotiate computers from other departments is to ask to "borrow" them for a while, without actually formally requesting a transfer of ownership. Periodically ask for extensions of the loan, and you'll probably never have to give the computers back.
- Watch the classified ads. Often the prices for Apple II's are very reasonable, especially for computers that aren't in working order. Most Apple II repairs are quite inexpensive, and you may be able to have your school district's computer staff do the repairs—or at least pay for them.

While you're locating all the free or low-cost computers you can find, begin your search for funds for additional equipment and software. You should have a complement of dedicated units—the rhythm- and pitch-training devices that will extend your personal teaching capacity—and you'll need software to make all those Apples you tracked down smart enough to teach music!

If your departmental budget isn't up to the strain, where do you go? Who has the funds? Your district almost certainly has a computer coordinator. Today, this person is usually in control of who gets the district's computer and software money. Find that person, and convince him or her that (1) you know what you want to do, and (2) what you want to do is important. Then get savvy about the politics of your district: find out who needs to be lobbied and *lobby them.*

To help convince nonmusicians, order some sample programs on a preview basis and stage a demonstration of the learning experiences your students will have. Many suppliers are willing to send demonstration copies of their software programs—some will even loan their hardware for preview. Also, be sure to keep up with what's happening in the field by attending conferences sponsored by MENC and its state affiliates. Companies from the music industry put on exhibits at nearly all of these meetings just so we can show you our exciting products firsthand. Come and see us!

Music Literacy

Finally, I'd like to offer an idea that's really a general caution to music educators: Cost is one fundamental issue, of course, but as we've discussed, there are always ways around it. An even bigger problem will be our attitude about technology in general, and technology as it specifically relates to the music curriculum. Traditionally, we music teachers have tended to work in isolation—not only from other departments but even from each other. We haven't always planned together well enough to reach a strong consensus as to what a music curriculum ought to include. We haven't developed a linear curriculum that will have students emerging from their elementary through high school years as literate musicians. Without this kind of thinking and planning, all that we have left to work on is performance. Performance is wonderful, of course, but there is much more to music, and we should be teaching it!

Right now—*today*—we're sitting in the middle of a technology revolution that enables us to teach a thoroughly grounded curriculum of music literacy. Manufacturers have produced hardware and software that will work together on the time-consuming task of presenting and providing practice with literacy skills while we continue to produce the outstanding performing groups our schools and communities want. And using these resources will make it even easier to produce those performances with musically literate students.

So the key to our success will be the curriculum we teach. As an encouragement for you to bring computers and technology into your music classrooms, some manufacturers produce useful planning materials that you can obtain, often at little or no cost, to help you in organizing your school and district music curriculum. These materials can help ensure that your students will not only develop specific musical performance skills but also undergo a sequence of music literacy development that will help them to emerge from their school program as whole musicians.

This is an absolutely fantastic time to be a music teacher. Go after your new technology assistants today—your students can't wait!

Selected Industry Sources

Alfred Publishing Co., Inc.; Julia Frazer, Marketing Director, or Andrew Surmani; 16380 Roscoe Boulevard, PO Box 10003, Van Nuys, CA 91410, telephone 818-891-5999.

Coda Music Software (division of Wenger Corporation); 1401 E. 79th Street, Minneapolis, MN 55425, telephone 612-854-1288.

Electronic Courseware Systems; David Peters, President, or Jodie Swaney, Sales; 1210 Lancaster Drive, Champaign, IL 61821, telephone 217-359-7099.

Korg USA, Inc.; Lee Whitmore, Product Manager, Home Products; 89 Frost Street, Westbury, NY 11590, telephone 516-333-9100.

Maestro Music, Inc.; Sharon Kunitz or Jim Kunitz; 2403 San Mateo, N.E., Suite P-12, Albuquerque, NM 87110, telephone 505-881-9181.

Music Systems for Learning, Inc.; Mary Jane DeGenaro; 311 East 38th Street, Suite 20C, New York, NY 10016, telephone 212-661-6096.

Piano Partners; Margaret Waldmann or Judy Gechwind; 521 E. 72nd Street, Suite 3A, New York, NY 10021, telephone 212-628-3912.

Pygraphics; Py Kolb or Cayleen Kolb; PO Box 63, Grapevine, TX 76051, telephone 800-222-7536.

Roland Corporation US; Larry Harms, Joy Carden, or Nancy Kewin; 7200 Dominion Circle, Los Angeles, CA 90040, telephone 213-685-5141.

Temporal Acuity Products, Inc.; Roger McRea, President, or Diane McRea, Vice President; 300 120th Avenue, N.E., Building 1, Suite 200, Bellevue, WA 98005, telephone 800-426-2673.

Yamaha Music Corporation USA; Joel Kabakov, Director of Institutional Development, Academic and Performing Arts, Keyboard Division; 6600 Orangethorpe Avenue, Buena Park, CA 90620, telephone 714-522-9239.

Many music educators produce compositions and books that would be of great interest to a large number of people—if the materials could only be published. Composers and writers, following a few commonsense procedures for the submission and development of their work, can successfully collaborate with publishers.

How to Get Your Music Published

by Sandy Feldstein

As a composer, arranger, and author, and as president and chief executive officer of CPP/Belwin, Inc. (formerly Columbia Pictures Publishing), one of the questions that I am asked most frequently is "How do I get my music published?" Although there is no one correct answer to this question, there are some basic ideas and concepts I can offer that will be helpful to you in getting your first piece of music or your first book accepted for publication.

One of the most important things to do is to try to picture the people who are going to make the final decision about accepting your manuscript. In most publishing companies, these people perform many functions—selecting materials is only one part of their job. On top of their other daily functions, they probably receive ten to thirty manuscripts for review each week. The sheer volume of material implies that the main, common sense goal that an author should have is to *make it easy for the publisher to review your material.* The following suggestions are all designed to meet that goal.

Making Contact

Send a letter describing your manuscript or manuscripts and

Sandy Feldstein is president and CEO of CPP/Belwin, Inc.

ask if the publisher is interested in the type of material you have available. Enclose a stamped, self-addressed postcard that can be conveniently checked off and returned to you. It should give the publisher a place to check if he is interested in reviewing your manuscript and if he would like you to submit it. Let's assume you receive the card back and the publisher indicates an interest in reviewing your work. Now comes the big question: what should you submit and how should you send it. All submissions should be accompanied by a letter. The letter should cover three specific points:

- *The reason you are submitting this particular manuscript to this publisher.* For example, it may be that this company publishes material that is similar to yours, and you feel that your piece would fit well into their catalog. Or, just the opposite, you feel that this publisher does not presently publish in this area and your composition or book would be a natural extension of their present program.
- *Why you wrote the composition or book.* For example, you can't find any books that teach this particular topic to young students, or you have been searching for an arrangement of this folk song for your elementary choir and cannot find any on the market.
- *Why you feel your manuscript should be published.* For example, "I have been using this book successfully with my students for three years, and many of my fellow teachers have expressed an interest in having copies of it. I'm sure this is an indication of how it would be received by other educators if it were available in published form." Your manuscript should also be accompanied by a brief résumé stating your musical and teaching experiences and other related points that are applicable to your career. This will give the publisher an idea of whether you attend a lot of conventions, feel capable of speaking to audiences, can be a guest conductor, can do clinics, and so on.

Finally, it is helpful if you only submit to one publisher at a time. Tell the publisher that you are not submitting your manuscript to another publisher simultaneously, but that if he is not interested, you would appreciate a prompt reply so you can submit elsewhere. Most editors dislike wasting time reviewing materials only to find out that someone else is reviewing the same piece and has made a decision the day before. You must remember that everyone's time is valuable.

Submitting Your Work

As to the manuscript itself, remember to prepare it neatly. Nothing is more frustrating to an editor than a sloppy manuscript. No one has the time to decipher hieroglyphics. Picture yourself looking at a pile of fifteen to twenty manuscripts; some are neat, clear, and easy to read, and some are sloppy and difficult to analyze. If you were the editor, which would you look at first? Taping score pages together or adding a simple binding to a manuscript can make it much easier to handle and more inviting for the editor to pick up and review.

All performance music should be submitted with a complete score and a tape or other recording of the work. This need not be a professional recording, but the editor will find it much quicker to listen to a piece first than to condense the score at the piano. If the publisher has an interest in your music after listening to the tape, he or she will go through your manuscript note by note. Books should, whenever possible, be submitted in their entirety. If a book manuscript is not complete, a table of contents and three sample chapters should be submitted.

For your protection, put a copyright notice on the first page of your manuscript. All you need to do is put a c in a circle (©) followed by the date and your name. It is not necessary to file your work with the copyright office in Washington, D.C., to protect your copyright.

Enclose a self-addressed, stamped postcard that asks the publisher to note the date your manuscript was received. When the publisher returns it to you, it will acknowledge receipt of your manuscript. This card should also ask when you should expect to hear from the publisher regarding a decision. Remember ... be patient. It often takes a great deal of time for a publisher to get to all of the manuscripts submitted for review. In addition, some publishers like you to enclose a self-addressed, stamped envelope for the return of the manuscript.

Practical Hints

If you know somebody who is involved with the publisher, don't be afraid to *use your connections*. A publisher is reluctant to be abrupt with the student of one of its authors or a friend of a music dealer. Along the same lines, attend conventions and try to meet publishers' representatives personally. A face tied to a name and a reminder that you have met is always helpful.

In general, do your homework and get to know about the publisher. Beside visiting the publisher's display at conventions, write for catalogs, go to the library, and browse in music stores. Check the listings of publishers in the Music Industry Conference guide, published every two or three years in the *Music Educators Journal* (see the March 1988 issue). Talk to local music dealers about various publishers: music dealers can be very helpful in guiding you to the most appropriate publisher.

Above all, don't get discouraged. For every manuscript accepted for publication there are hundreds of good ones rejected. A rejection may not relate to the music itself but be the result of a combination of timing, past commitments, the economy, and a host of other variables that are outside your control.

Most of these ideas are common sense and based on one main goal—making the publishing decision easy for the editor or editors. If you incorporate these ideas into your approach, you will have a better chance of having your manuscript reviewed conscientiously and in depth. The future of music and music educators is strongly dependent on the materials available to perform and to learn from. The constant influx of new ideas and new creators is essential for the growth of all mankind, so don't get discouraged. I hope some of these ideas are helpful in getting your music and books published.

The Publishing Process

What can you expect if you are successful and a publisher accepts your manuscript? First, you should know that a manuscript is rarely published "as is." Often the publisher accepts the manuscript with certain provisions or suggestions. For example, "We are very interested in publishing this band composition, but from measures 58–64 the tessitura of the trombones change this grade two composition to grade four. We would like you to rethink and rewrite those measures to keep the entire piece at a grade two level."

When a book is submitted, a publisher may ask you to include another chapter on a topic that wasn't covered in your original draft. Obviously, all suggestions or requests are just that. If you don't agree, you should discuss the reasons for your disagreement with your publisher. When the manuscript is corrected or adjusted, it will go back to the publisher to be prepared for production. At this point, you will receive a contract. The contract is a legal document wherein you assign the copyright of your creation to the publisher. It defines, among other things, how you will be compensated for your work.

If you are publishing a musical composition, it will be prepared for engraving by music editors and will be engraved by the publisher. You, as the composer, will proofread the engravings to be sure that they are perfect (most publishers also have the music proofread by a a professional proofreader). Any questions from the proofreader will be communicated to you, and the combined corrections will be made before a composition goes to print.

Obviously, a book is a little more complex. Artwork, diagrams, and interior design are all involved. Accompanying cassettes, records, compact discs, or videotapes may need to be produced. All in all, it is a time-consuming process that involves a great deal of interaction between the publisher and the creator.

Once the music or book is printed, it must be promoted. As the author, you may well be involved in this aspect of the publicity process. Guest conducting, attending conventions, and doing presentations to schools and to music dealers may all be part of the plan.

All in all, it is an exciting and rewarding area to be involved in. As I said before, don't get discouraged. If you feel you have something to say, keep saying it, and eventually someone will hear you.

The excitement of seeing your first piece or book published is only surpassed by seeing your second work in print, and each new one becomes the most important. Creating music and books for publication is one of those rare employment opportunities: one that can add to the growth and enjoyment of human beings while affording the creator financial remuneration. The music community needs your contributions.

The current copyright law of the United States developed out of a series of compromises between the needs of authors and publishers to protect their work and the needs of music educators and others to have practical access to the intellectual products that shape our society. Charles Gary presents a view of the history of the law's development and explains some of the law's implications for the classroom and the rehearsal hall.

Working within the Copyright Law

by Charles Gary

Back in the late 1960s and early 1970s, the Congressional Judiciary Committee asked representatives of teachers and representatives of the publishers to meet together to see if we couldn't iron out our differences with respect to the proposed changes in the copyright law. The differences were quite sizable, and there was a period when it appeared that we were at an impasse—that we were not going to make any progress whatsoever. It was then that the music publishers and the music educators (who knew each other so well from working together cooperatively on conventions and programs of various sorts) were able to demonstrate to the rest of the group that it was feasible for us to make some compromises. We went on and were able to come up with something that Congress eventually passed into law.

When that happened, in 1976, two music publishers' associations asked me to go around to meetings of music educators and explain the law to them. I found that, at that time, the teachers' first reaction to the subject of copyright was, "Oh, this is something that is going to tell me what I can't do!" In other words, they were predisposed to be negative about the whole operation. I felt that one of the things I had to do was to convince them that Congress had done us a real favor in passing this law, because it

---

Charles Gary is a consultant to the Music Publishers' Association.

clarified so many things that were hazy. I will try, in this brief discussion, to explain to you what some of those clarifications mean.

Background

There is nothing new about copyright. In fact, we've had a copyright law since 1790, when it became the tenth law to be passed by our first Congress. The purpose of this law, of course, was to encourage the creative members of society to write music, to write poetry, to write books, and to invent things— and it has worked very well for the benefit of all of us. We do not live in 1790, however, so there have had to be revisions of the law from time to time; one in 1831, another in 1870, one in 1909, and then this last major change in 1976. In 1989, the law was further amended as the result of the United States joining the Berne Convention. Penalties were also increased in an attempt to halt the pirating of computer programs. The period between major changes in the law, from 1909 to 1976, was a period in which there was probably more change in our society than at any other time in the two hundred years of our history.

There were many things that had to be looked at in preparing the revised law, but the purpose of the law remains the same: to protect the creator and to encourage creativity. To do that, section 106 of the law gives the creator five exclusive rights. These are to reproduce the work (in other words, to make copies), to prepare derivative works (in our case, to make arrangements), to distribute the work (to sell it, rent it, or lease it), to perform the work publicly, and finally to display the work. But there have always been limitations to those rights— for instance, the temporal limitation: how long does this right last? Originally, it was a very short period— something like ten years. Over the years it has been extended— under the 1909 law, it was twenty-eight years, a period that was renewable for another twenty-eight years. This is one of the things that caused a great deal of discussion as we considered the new law. The publishers were very anxious to have the United States law be the same as that of the rest of the world, which protects the work from its creation for the remainder of the life of the creator plus fifty years.

When the educators saw how much this meant to the publishers, they were able to use it as a bargaining chip. They said, "We will give you life plus fifty if you will give us some of the things we feel it is necessary to have as teachers." And it worked out that way. One of the problems with life plus fifty, of course, is what was to be done with the things that are already protected over a potential fifty-six year period from the date of creation? The Congress settled this by arbitrarily picking a seventy-five-year period and saying everything that was under copyright on the date of the law's passage would remain protected for seventy-five years from the initial date of copyright and then go into the public domain. That means that everything that was copyrighted in 1914 went into the public domain on December 31, 1989.

Penalties

The most important other new parts of the law have to do with remedies for infringement (the penalties for people who break the law) and a section called "fair use." Penalties are kind of nasty, so let's get them out of the way. They say that if there is an infringement, the judge must fine the infringer not less than $500—and he or she may raise it to as high as $20,000. If it is willful infringement, meaning that the person who broke the law knew he was breaking the law and went ahead and did it anyway, the total could be as much as $100,000 for each infringement. If it is willful infringement for gain, the fine can be as much as $100,000 plus two years' imprisonment. This means, if you were to make copies of all of the numbers you were doing on your next program and there were ten numbers on the program, you might be liable for a million-dollar fine.

However, the judge is instructed that if you can convince him or her that you were not aware that what you were doing was an infringement of the law, the minimum penalty may be reduced to $200—*may be* reduced.

Fair Use

Certain members of society—teachers, scholars, critics, and researchers—are covered under a special provision called "fair use." That provision tells the judge that if you plead fair use and are successful in convincing him or her that you thought what you were doing was fair use, the judge shall reduce the fine to zero. It seems obvious when you belong to a group that is given such a special protection as this, you had better know what it's all about.

Until the 1976 law, there was nothing written down about fair use; it was what any judge wished to say it was. If the judge ruled that he or she was not going to fine an individual because—in that judge's opinion—what the individual did was fair use, that individual could go scot-free. On the other hand, a judge in a neighboring state might rule that another teacher was guilty for doing exactly the same thing. There were no criteria for the judges to use as guidelines; so one of the prime objectives of the education group was to get statutory fair use—in other words, to get the concept of fair use written into the law. Congress was very obliging on their first round with a law. They came back and said that fair use of copyrighted material shall not be considered an infringement, period. Our response was, "Thank you very much, but what does it mean? We don't know anything more than we knew before because nobody still knows what fair use is." They said, "We have no idea. You tell us." So they put us all—publishers, teachers, librarians, and scholars—into a hot room with no air conditioning over in the Library of Congress one summer afternoon, and said, "You decide what the criteria for fair use should be."

After considerable wrangling, we came up with four criteria that Congress would accept. The first was the purpose and the character of the use: What is it that you propose to do with this piece of protected material? Is it going to be for commercial use or is it for educational use? The second criterion was the nature of the copyrighted work: is it a textbook, is it a workbook, is it a test, is it an epic poem, an art song, a limerick, a novel, or an opera? The third criterion was based on the extent of use: How much are you using and how important is the portion of it that you are using? And, of course, how many copies are being made?

The last criterion was an economic concern: what is the effect on the potential market for the work or its value? The creator was given an exclusive right to protect his creative work in order to encourage him or her; the sale of the work, of course, would be one of the ways the creator might be expected to find encouragement. If what you were doing was going to damage the creator's potential market, that was considered to be a very important criterion for deciding whether it was a fair use or not.

The other important thing about fair use is that all four of these criteria must be applied. You can't say, for instance, that "it's an educational use, therefore it's fair use." Or you can't say, "But I'm using such a small portion of it that it really doesn't matter—I ought to be allowed to do whatever I want to with fifteen seconds of a two-hour composition." We had as a counsel to the ad hoc group a very dear man, Harry Rosenfield, who once made this point in front of the group by saying, "Supposing you wanted to use the opening motive from Beethoven's Fifth Symphony to sell shoes, and it was still in copyright? Beethoven would have a right to object, because in taking those four notes you have taken the essence of his symphony."

These four criteria were accepted by the Judiciary Committee of the House and were written into the bill. The law rocked along over several Congresses, as a matter of fact, because they would get busy with something else and not finish the bill—it would never go forward. These four criteria, however, stayed in each version of the bill as it was introduced to a new Congress. Then, as we got close to finalizing the bill and it looked like it was going to go to President Ford for signature, both the publishers and the educators got worried that maybe this wasn't specific enough. And so we asked Congress, "Couldn't you give us some further details?" Once again, they said to us, "You do it!"

As a result, two sets of guidelines were prepared: one for copyrighted music materials and the other for copyrighted books and periodicals. These guidelines were examples of the kind of thing that both sides agreed should be allowable. For example, the first music guideline allows "emergency copying to replace purchase copies which for any reason are not available for an imminent performance, provided replacement copies shall be substituted in due course." This would mean that if someone loses his or her music for a concert, you could make copies from the music for one of the other stands and let everyone perform with the group (rather than losing a whole stand for the concert). Instead of putting the photocopies back in the file, however, you are instructed to purchase replacement copies. Teachers frequently raise the point that they don't have the money to do that. Well, it isn't your responsibility to do it—you didn't lose them. If the board is wealthy enough that they can afford to buy the replacement copies, fine. If not, it is the responsibility of the student who lost the music—it certainly wasn't the composer's fault.

The second guideline is quite a mouthful; to understand it, I suggest that you read it for yourself in one of the MENC or Music Publishers' Association publications about copyright. In essence, the guideline says that you can make multiple copies of not more than 10 percent of a copyrighted work to use for classroom discussion (but not for performance purposes). For example, if you want to discuss the voice leading in an eight-bar progression of some modern composer's work as a harmony exercise, you could give everyone in the class a copy of the music as long as the part you copied was not more than 10 percent of the work.

The third criterion gives you the right to edit or simplify purchased copies that you own, because it is considered that that is part of your professional duty. There may be a time when you need to alter the tenor part because the tessitura is just too high for your young boys. There may be a time when you need to take out some notes because your children have not developed the skills to play all the sixteenth notes, but they could play the passage in eighth notes. So the guideline says that you are given the right to make those alterations "as long as it doesn't ruin the general impression that the composer had, i.e., the fundamental character of the work." By the way, no lyrics may be altered, and no lyrics may be added if none exist.

The fourth criterion says that a single recording of a performance by students may be made for evaluation or rehearsal purposes and may be retained by the educational institution or individual teacher. This is a provision that we use in the universities to keep a copy of graduate recitals; it provides a record similar to a copy of a student's master's thesis. A number of years ago, when I was operating a copyright information booth at the MENC conference in Miami, I had a man argue with me saying that one copy is not enough—it should read two copies in the law. But I said that is not what Congress approved: they approved a single copy and there is nothing I can do about it. If one copy doesn't satisfy your needs, write your congressman or get special permission from the copyright holder.

After an all-day meeting in Washington in which we drafted those four guidelines, I flew back to Purdue, where I was teaching at the time, and found a note on my desk that read, "make out the music history exam." What I intended to do was to put a number of excerpts from the recordings we held in our library onto a tape so that I just had to punch one button and play the listening exam rather than put the disks on a turntable and try and find the right grooves. I called the members of the music publishing industry who were on the committee and suggested that we needed something to cover this use; so we have a fifth guideline: a single copy of a sound recording may be made from sound recordings owned by the educational institution for oral exercises or examinations.

There is a parenthetical statement in this guideline that says this covers only the copyright of the music and not any copyright that might exist on the sound recording. This is because we just could not get the recording industry to agree to this provision. You should know that recordings before 1972 were not copyrightable in this country, but for any recordings you have that were made after 1972, the recordings as well as the music itself are probably copyrighted.

Prohibitions and Classroom Use

I have mentioned that this was a game of compromise; so, along with those five uses that teachers can make of copyrightable material there are five prohibitions. You may not copy to create an anthology. You may not copy from works intended to be consumable, like workbooks, exercises, standardized tests, and answer sheets. You may not copy for the purpose of performance except as covered by that business of the lost copy. You may not copy for the purpose of substituting for the purchase of music, and you may not copy without inclusion of any copyright notice that appears on the printed copy. You can get forms for requesting permission to arrange, or to inquire about out-of-print music, from the Music Publishers' Association, 130 West 57th Street, New York 10019. They will also send you "A Practical Outline," which covers many of these points.

The guidelines that the classroom teachers worked out with the book publishers are somewhat similar. For example, teachers may make single copies of a chapter from a book, an article from a periodical or a newspaper, a short story or a poem, a chart, a diagram, a drawing, or a cartoon. In addition, teachers can make multiple copies for classroom use under certain conditions. The first condition is that the copy meets the test of brevity and spontaneity.

The guideline's definitions of "brevity" and "spontaneity" are lawyers' definitions, and are therefore not brief. In a nutshell, however, you may copy, as fair use, a poem if it is less than 250 words, a prose work of less than 2,500 words, or an excerpt from a prose work of not more than 1,000 words, or 10 percent of the work, whichever is less. The concept of spontaneity is important because it brings out the idea that we want teachers to be creative and we don't want this law to keep them from doing the best teaching they know how to do. The Congress was trying to permit things that teachers need to do on the spur of the moment—what we began to refer to as "the teachable moment." A supervisor who observed such a use, however, could not write a directive to all the teachers under his or her supervision and tell them to use copyrighted material in this way—that would not be permissible.

The law also contains some limitations as to how much copying you can do from one source. For instance, one of the guidelines reads: there shall be no more than nine instances of such multiple copying for one course during one class term.

Teachers ought to feel very good about the 1976 version of the copyright law; they were given some very specific things that they were allowed to do because they *are* teachers. These are things that nobody else can do. But whenever you define anything, it places limits—so it not only says what you can do, but it makes it very clear what you cannot do. Some find that a little onerous. But that is the law; that is what Congress has decided is best for the country.

1505-10-2M-3/90